HazelelizabethlillliecheeirmavelladolllizziecorineevanellLavernebettyjovoncillemah
jivancemakaylakendallshellyadairadajahchristiechriskhaliakanishatanishadarlaed
ythtashajessiesandralouisedeanaanayaminniemaelilllianartimeseloraellenrhodaka
therinemalissaconnieconstanceelieeleanorconstancevirginiabonnieannesuekaye
sthergloriamariechristineharrietlindaashantijacquelinejohnniemaeversalindanicol
epathelenangelabeatricerebamarybrendavirginiacheecheerachaeltanyajoettalelali
sacarolejeannienatalielauriecandydoramaudiearmenterarlenalillietheomaelynnvic
toriaseawellowEdithgwendolynjeanjunerillastephaniediannmittiebeatricemarjoryir
enerebeccalouiseruthMildredythionediannannebeverlybarbararosemarylolamikkik
atiemariettadorthatheomaellenmarciajeanalleasjaninelisakarenmariedarenedarrita
marierolandasharonlynneleeannanadeansherylzeolareginaphylliskristajanievelma
floreenjessielorettaleveniarenabernettaanitabrendaangelaantionettecamelladebra
cherimaryreneesusiejackiejudylelalilliemozellmelindamoszellleoliasheilarobinshir
leyminniejoannnancyfanniecarolynrosadebbierubyjewellesesnepatricepeggyemil
yclarahopehelencynthiagracelizziemaelouannienelliejunehazelmargaretemmabett
yjoycelougeniamarilynsammiegeraldinekathilliandeborahzeofiouscookieelouisei
damelanieveranannielisheyd **She** hthelmamarthacharleneodessamablepatri
ciashawnstaceyfrancestwiladd **She** neleonavenusernestineanniec
hristinemelindatracypaulaapliscecilianicolekatrinacharlottejud
ithbethjosephineoneidamanetamarashannonmahjililnarob
inpaulabonniestellareginalisaviolaeloiseoliviadeniseleolapanziegoldyne
stellareginalisaviolaeloiseoliviadeniseleolapanziesarahadagoldyneoleathatiffanya
gnessonyacalliecoralavernemahjijanicekathrynloisjohnnieflorenceangeleeberthac
armalethajrilorraineonedavirgielindanorawinonalenamalverbernicegloriaplulavivia
ndoriselainevenice irmabessiedarleneprincesspaulinepennyveradorethabonniegra
cequeensusanjuanitamyrtlejosieritajanecheryloliveoliviarosettatreasureethellydial
oveymargueritedanamonamattiesuzettecarolroxannesandranolavoncillemakaylav
ernillaednamamiejuliecladairmakathleencelestinelilliealmaelmaelsiebilliecharlese
ttaelinoraloraellenrhodavaloniamargaretdeloresgladysjacquelineeleanorjettiearie
diannejozeldazellacamillealbertajevianpriscillaloistheolaelaineconsueloheatherja
ninemurielhenriettaasacarrieevelynkristineevaeveaccleconstancenormaandreatre
ssachelsealynetteserrenablanchedonnageorgiaanitaesthhersandyeddiemarianyol
andaclaudiachriswandadaisydoviephebealvasameliabonitacarmentanyadorafloss
ierivianhattiesammielorettainasandragaylevaldagussieminniesabrinanellvickieeu
niceadrienneorebajeanetteaddiequanettabeckyaudreyelizabethsharonveronicavia
nnarlenaclaricelorileahelaramichellejulieroselynmattiemariaaltaangelavaloriadar
lanaomiaugustajanicegertrudeceatriaelnorapamelavigeneolajeannieaprilloreneros
iedenisetsitsimonicaabigaildelphiamatrisnarvaleewandaviestaramonakristalonnie
pattykaysojournersadiephillisgwenmalverfreddierickoledawnvirginiacececeljessieh
arrietcolleenbeulahhannahkatricestarlacosundratrudygenevagenaysylviamartinan
elliegerthreenjuliadorcasdemetriadeborahfloradellaolivejoannamarjmalikaconniek
iangalauriesheliamagdalenemiriansheba jemimahkaylacheyennephoebevashtiJoet
talelalisacarolejeannienatalielauriecandydoramaudiearmenterarlenalillietheomael
ynnvictoriaseawellowEdithgwendjunerillastephaniediannmittiebeatricem
arjoryirenerebecrosemarylol
calouiseruth Mildredythionediabarbararosemarylol

Blac Louinsen TN   Miam Kenensw FL

authorHOUSE™

AuthorHouse™
1663 Liberty Drive, Suite 200
Bloomington, IN 47403
www.authorhouse.com
Phone: 1-800-839-8640

AuthorHouse™ UK Ltd.
500 Avebury Boulevard
Central Milton Keynes, MK9 2BE
www.authorhouse.co.uk
Phone: 08001974150

First published by AuthorHouse 4/21/2009

ISBN: 978-1-4184-6470-7 (e)
ISBN: 978-1-4184-4473-0 (sc)

Library of Congress Control Number: 2002108232

Printed in the United States of America
Bloomington, Indiana

This book is printed on acid-free paper.

*These few chosen words are dedicated
to all the Shes in my lifeline....
starting with Eve in the Cradle of Civilization
and including all the Shes on this Dedication Page*

She lives

She lives long and strong
Reclining at the table
Thou hast prepared for her
Dining with a potpourri of personalities
She endures new, but old stories
While the sands of time
Tic-tocks a tacit bittersweet melody
In the ageless tunnel of time.

Her face is lined with illustrations
Of a sweet, sweet, slice of life
Spiced, spiked, and seasoned with the
Fruit of the Spirit . . .
Love, joy, peace, patience,
Gentleness, kindness, goodness,
Faithfulness, and self-control
She is our lifeline
Sprinkling each rite of passage
With a blending of wisdom, wit, and wise
Listen intently
She carries lessons of life
In her soul.

The Versatility of Feminity . . .

Bathed, blushed, and blessed
In the sprinkling glow of
History's flow.

Time and She . . . .

Time and she
Bride and groom
Inseparable
Came into the vineyard
Dawn to dusk
Labored and toiled.

Seasons aged
Intertwined with
Wisdom, wit and wise.

Time and tide
Now inseparable
Carrying the mysterious torch
Christened Eternity.

She murmurs
O hear my hushed cry
Harken to my peaceful plea
Lay me down to Eternity
Let all who love
Embrace and kiss my
Sweet and silent memory.

HazelelizabethlilliecheeirmavelladolllizziecorineevanellLavernebettyjovoncillemah
jivancemakaylakendallshellyadairadajahchristiechriskhaliakanishatanishadarlaed
ythtashajessiesandralouisedeanaanayaminniemaelillianartimeseloraellenrhodaka
therinemalissaconnieconstanceelieeleanorconstancevirginiabonnieannesuekaye
sthergloriamariechristineharrietlindaashantijacquellnejohnniemaeversalindanicol
epathelenangelabeatricerebamarybrendavirginiacheecheerachaeltanyajoettalelali
sacarolejeannienatalielauriecandydoramaudiearmenterarlenalillietheomaelynnvic
toriaseawellowEdithgwendolynjeanjunerillastephaniediannmittiebeatricemarjoryir
enerebeccalouiseruthMildredythionediannannebeverlybarbararosemarylolamikkik
atiemariettadorthatheomaellenmarciajeanalleasjaninelisakarenmariedarenedarrita
marierolandasharonlynneleeannanadeansherylzeolareginaphylliskristajanievelma
floreenjessielorettaleveniarenabernettaanitabrendaangelaantionettecamelladebra
cherimaryreneesusiejackiejudylelalilliemozellmelindamoszellleoliasheilarobinshir
leyminniejoannnancyfanniecarolynrosadebbierubyjewellesesnepatricepeggyemil
yclarahopehelencynthiagracelizziemaelouannienelliejunehazelmargaretemmabett
yjoycelougeniamarilynsammiegeraldinekathililliandeborahzeofiouscookieelouisei
damelanieverannanielisheydorothylesliethelmamarthacharleneodessamablepatri
ciashawnstaceyfrancestwiladoramalvinawilliepearlineleonavenusernestineanniec
hristinemelindatracypaulaaplislucillekarenidarebacecilianicolekatrinacharlottejud
ithbethjosephineoneidamarvalavernekimberlymaxinetamarashannonmahjililnarob
inpaulabonniestellareginalisaviolaeloiseoliviadeniseleolapanziegoldyne
stellareginalisaviolaeloiseoliviadeniseleolapanziesarahadagoldyneoleathatiffanya
gnessonyacalliecoralavernemahjijanicekathrynloisjohnnieflorenceangeleeberthac
armalethajrilorraineonedavirgielindanorawinonalenamalverberniceglorialulavivia
ndoriselaineveniceirmabessiedarleneprincesspaulinepennyveradorethabonniegra
cequeensusanjuanitamyrtlejosieritajanecheryloliveoliviarosettatreasureethellydial
oveymarqueritedanamonamattiesuzettecarolroxannesandranolavoncillemakaylav
ernillaednamamiejuliecladairmakathleencelestinelilliealmaelmaelsiebilliecharlese
ttaelinoraloraellenrhodavaloniamargaretdeloresgladysjacquelineeleanorjettiearie
diannejozeldazellacamillealbertajevianpriscillaloistheolaelaineconsueloheatherja
ninemurielhenriettaasacarrieevelynkristineevaeveaccleconstancenormaandreatre
ssachelsealynetteserrenablanchedonnageorgiaanitaesthhersandyeddiemarianyol
andaclaudiachriswandadaisydoviephebealvasameliabonitacarmentanyadorafloss
ierivianhattiesammielorettainasandragaylevaldagussieminniesabrinanellvickieeu
niceadrienneorebajeanetteaddiequanettabeckyaudreyelizabethsharonveronicavia
nnarlenaclaricelorileaheklaramichellejulieroselynmattiemariaaltaangelavaloriadar
lanaomiaugustajanicegertrudeceatriaelnorapamelavigeneolajeannieaprilloreneros
iedenisetsitsimonicaabigaildelphiamatrisnarvaleewandaviestaramonakristalonnie
pattykaysojournersadiephillisgwenmalverfreddierickoledawnvirginiaceceljessieh
arrietcolleenbeulahhannahkatricestarlacosundratrudygenevagenaysylviamartinan
elliegerthreenjuliadorcasdemetriadeborahfloradellaolivejoannamarjmalikaconniek
iangalaurieshelliamagdalenemirianshebajemimahkaylacheyennephoebevashtiJoet
talelalisacarolejeannienatalielauriecandydoramaudiearmenterarlenalillietheomael
ynnvictoriaseawellowEdithgwendolynjeanjunerillastephaniediannmittiebeatricem
arjoryirenerebeccalouiseruthMildredythionediannannebeverlybarbararosemarylol

Table of Contents

HazelelizabethlilliecheeirmavelladolllizziecorineevanellLavernebettyjovoncillemah
jivancemakaylakendallshellyadairadajahchristiechriskhaliakanishatanishadarlaed
ythtashajessiesandralouisedeanaanayaminniemaelillianartimeseloraellenrhodaka
therinemalissaconnieconstanceelieeleanorconstancevirginiabonnieannesuekaye
sthergloriamariechristineharrietlindaashantijacquelinejohnniemaeversalindanicol
epathelenangelabeatricerebamarybrendavirginiacheecheerachaeltanyajoettalelali
sacarolejeannienatalielauriecandydoramaudiearmenterarlenalillietheomaelynnvic
toriaseawellowEdithgwendolynjeanjunerillastephaniediannmittiebeatricemarjoryir
enerebeccalouiseruthMildredythionediannannebeverlybarbararosemarylolamikkik
atiemariettadorthatheomaellenmarciajeanalleasjaninelisakarenmariedarenedarrita
marierolandasharonlynneleeannanadeansherylzeolareginaphylliskristajanievelma
floreenjessielorettaleveniarenabernettaanitabrendaangelaantionettecamelladebra
cherimaryreneesusiejackiejudylelalilliemozellmelindamoszellleoliasheilarobinshir
leyminniejoannnancyfanniecarolynrosadebbierubyjewellesesnepatricepeggyemil
yclarahopehelencynthiagracelizziemaelouannienelliejunehazelmargaretemmabett
yjoycelougeniamarilynsammiegeraldinekathililliandeborahzeofiouscookieeelouisei
damelanieverananielisheydorothylesliethelmamarthacharleneodessamablepatri
ciashawnstacey**SISTAHS**ouernestineanniec
hristinemelindatracyp**S**sen**I**s**T**areni**A**a**H**ccilia**S**olekat**j**nacharlottejud
ithbethjosephineolleidamarvalavernekimberlymaxinetamarashannonmahjililnarob
inpaulabonniestellareginalisaviolaeloiseoliviadeniseleolapanziegoldyne
stellareginalisaviolaeloiseolivia**ARE**rahadagoldyneoleathatiffanya
gnessonyacalliecoralavernema**ARE**hryloisjohnnieflorenceangeleeberthac
armalethajrilorraineonedavir**ARE**elinda**C**ravon**C**halenamalverbernicegloriaIulaviia
ndoriselaineveniceirmabessiedarleneprincesspaulinepennyveradorethabonniegra
cequeensusanjuanitamyrtlejosieritajanecheryloliveoliviarosettatreasureethellydial
oveymargueritedanamonamattiesuzettecarolroxannesandranolavoncillemakaylav
ernillaednamamiejuliecladairmakathleencelestinelillliealmaelmaelsiebilliecharlese
ttaelinoraloraellenrhodavaloniamargaretdeloresgladysjacquelineeleanorjettiearie
diannejozeldazellacamillealbertajevianpriscillaloistheolaelaineconsueloheatherja
ninemurielhenriettaasacarrieevelynkristineevaeveaccleconstancenormaandreatre
ssachelsealynetteserrenablanchedonnageorgiaanitaesthhersandyeddiemarianyol
andaclaudiachriswandadaisydoviephebealvasameliabonitacarmentanyadorafloss
ierivianhattiesammielorettainasandragaylevaldagussieminniesabrinanellvickieeu
niceadrienneorebajeanetteaddiequanettabeckyaudreyelizabethsharonveronicavia
nnarlenaclaricelorileaheklaramichellejulieroselynmattiemariaaltaangelavaloriadar
lanaomiaugustajanicegertrudeceatriaelnorapamelavigeneolajeannieaprillloreneros
iedenisetsitsimonicaabigaildelphiamatrisnarvaleewandaviestaramonakristalonnie
pattykaysojournersadiephillisgwenmalverfreddierickoledawnvirginiaceceljessieh
arrietcolleenbeulahhannahkatricestarlacosundratrudygenevagenaysylviamartinan
elliegerthreenjuliadorcasdemetriadeborahfloradellaoliyejoannamarjmalikaconniek
iangalaurieshellamagdalenemiriamshebajemimahkaylacheyennephoebevashtiJoet
talelalisacarolejeannienatalielauriecandydoramaudiearmenterarlenalillietheomael
ynnvictoriaseawellowEdithgwendolynjeanjunerillastephaniediannmittiebeatricem
arjoryirenerebeccalouiseruthMildredythionediannannebeverlybarbararosemarylol

1

Sistahs are . . .

Visions of beauty
Miracles in motion
And money-order mamas

A sistah is a real, rich and rare deal
And so much more
She can dish it out, dole it out, and deliver extra value
. . . You always get more
Than you bargained for.

The hand she's dealt is always a winning one
'Cuz it's just a state of mind
Lots of lotto luck
Can whip whisk in a whopping way
Knows how to slam the trumps
As she talks that jive
And when she goes on a bingo binge
Wins enough for all her friends
Always got a stash of cash
And payday loans ain't in her path

She's always in the mood
No matter the groove
Her spirit will never leave you guessing
Rather you'll always go away with a binding impression

No body gets away messing with
Or messing up her stuff,
She'll deliver to you a tongue-lashing as powerful
As a Joe Louis/Muhammed Ali punch and
As quick and hot as a taste of the Tropics
Laced with Mama's hot barbeque sauce.

She's a high performance and high maintenance lady
A top-notch Sistah . . .
And I'm glad she's in my corner.

Who Is My Sistah?

She can be likened to a double-edged sword
Always on the cutting edge of things, thangs, and thoughts
Strong and sweet, takes no stuff
'Cuz she is the right stuff
Knows the donkey's braw
And will not fall into his hole
She will take on the world
When she believes she's right
Size and shape presents no barriers
From the ant to the elephant
She fears no obstacle
For she knows her steps are ordered
By one greater than she.

If you are a true sistah
You know I speak the truth
You will allow nary a soul
To push your panic button
Shove you in a hole
Or seize your pot of gold
Rain or shine, your word is your bond
And is as good as God's rainbow
For it comes from above.

A sistah will love you, but knows still
The limit and the value of self-control.

A sistah is a sistah is a sistah
She knows that somewhere over the rainbow
Awaits her reward . . . a pot of gold
And the joy of her journey
Is taking another sistah's hand
And helping her struggle
Up the rough side of the mountain
Making sure that she skips
And misses all the holes.

Thanks for being my sistah!

The Color of Love . . .

Black-eyed pea teasing tan, inlaid ivory
Seasoned and soothing spiced saffron
The depth of darkest black
Sweet, sweet coconut brown

My sistah, my sistahs,
Native and natural blush of Love

What is Love . . .

Thoughts that speak the quiet brilliance of onyx
A spellbinding and spirited smile
Blooming the blessings of precious pearls
A heart as high as Hope
And as good as gold

My sistah, my sistahs,
You are Love

You exude a touch and a tint of God's earthtone rainbow
Radiating the integrity of rubies and emeralds
You were delivered from fertile waters
Flowing with the strength of
Ruth, Deborah, Esther, Jemimah, Keziah, Keren-Happuch,
Tubman, Sojourner, Wheatley, Bethune
Your aunties, big mamas, and M'Dears

My sistahs, my sistah,
You are a minute in time
A moment of whispered intimacy
Between the sparkling dust of nature
And the breath of God

My sistah . . .
Forever and everyday
You are the Right Stuff!

Sistahs . . .

You are the salt and pepper in his shakers
The yeast in his bread
The butter on his biscuits
The jam and jelly spread all over his toast
The sugar in his triple layer coconut cake
The chocolate chips in his cookies
The red in his ice cold kool-aid
The hot, medium and mild sauce
Marinating his spare ribs.
Oh, how grinnin' glad
He oughta be
That God, whilst he lay sleeping
Took part of his inner beauty
And created a mate solely for him.

The sweet and sassy spice
In his slice of life.

. . . A Limited Edition . . .

All matter and substance purposed
From the finest array and assortment
Of God's goods.

Every detail of your being
Down to the last minuscule pore
Was created and fashioned
With immeasurable and profound
Love and care.

Your coloring
Fired in fertile dust
A silhouette
Designed rich and rare
Reflecting the Spirit of Light
Is true, correct, and balanced.

There is no need now or ever
To modify, alter, or change
A single solitary thing
Not even a single strand of hair.

Yes, you are a Limited Edition
Created by a silent stroke
Of the Artist Extra-ordinaire
The Master indeed . . .

Legitimate and exceptional
A work of art
A labor of love
A toil of tenderness
Created in the image
Of I Am, and christened
Beautiful and extraordinary
A one-of-a-kind masterpiece.

Miss Ribb

What a beautiful sight you ladies are
Every color of God's earth tone rainbow
Honey dripping hush, cool and mellow yellow, jungle juice jet black,
Coffee colored with whipping cream, pecan-flavored brown
And teasing bamboo tan
My, my, my, what a pretty picture you all sketch . . . and yo heads
Colored, wrapped, and draped in dos that are styled to stun and amaze
Waves, weaves, sidesweeps and upsweeps, long and finger-popping short
Ala naturale, shaved, cornrows, Madam C. J'd down
And water-slicked black, spit curls
Beaded braids tucked behind jeweled lobes
My my my, what a sight - illustrated and animated faces with
Sculpted bright red lips and matching rouged cheeks
Sparkling blue shadowed eyes neath arched brows
Winking and blinking, behind horned rimed glasses
M sistahs, my sistah, you are a magnificent spectacle
With a little round of gold poised and posed atop a broad nose
Necks collared and clad in silver, beads, and gold
Oh weeeeee, Mama, What a sight what a sight
Don't let me start on the clothes thang
Everything from authentic African to red, white, and blue, apple pie American
And yo own vogue, my sistahs,
You know how to breathe life in any kinda old rags and faded clothes
Color-coded, no nonsense style, grace, and beauty
That's my sistahs, turning fashion every which-a-way, but loose
From head to toe, front to back
No wonder, we're gawked at, envied and copied
But, the fact of the matter remains, my sistahs, we is tough, we is rough
Whatever the case, we are the natural sparkling dust of nature
And cannot be duplicated!
Cause undergirding it all, is the attitude
The way we walk and talk, the way the neck, hands, hips, and eyes act up in a Synchronized movement and motion that will tickle a tune on any eighty-eight Inciting a voice in the background saying, *give the drummer some*
Sistahs, we just so tough and naturally dressed up

That God is the only one who coulda fashioned fine brown frames like us
From a rib and allowed Adam to name us,
Mama, Baby, Sugar, Darling, Dear
And that little secret sweet nothin' name
that is often whispered in just yo ear
Sistahs, thank God for fixing Adam so he didn't miss that rib!
And brothers, put on your bib, savor your rib
It's spiced, salted, and seasoned specially for you
And all you others out there . . . Your eyes may shine
Your teeth may grit, but none of this will you git!

Ribs

It's amazing, but true
From dust God made me and you
Dubbed us unique
Colored us . . .
Chocolate choice, ebony elite
Mellow yellow, honey hush
Coifed and combed
Ala naturale every single strand
Looked the iris in the eye
Poked the lips out in a grin, giggle and a smile
Chided the chin not to have a twin
While he tucked the belly button in
Bonded nails to greasy fingers
And big and little corned toes too
Told the tendon, be sensitive to all heels
He laughed with the funny and
Kissed the marrow in our bones
Married all the parts
And told them to serve as one
Bled the life line in criss-cross paths and trails
All leading to the heart's content
It's amazing but true
From dust God made me and you
And even guaranteed us
A spot for hands on our hips
A place for ribs in a cage
Which came from Adam's spare.

There is Something Good . . .

There is something good on my mind that I just have to say . . .
It has everything to do with what happened on page one
A long time ago

But listen to this first . . .
Some say, oooo-weeeeeeeee man
This is sho-nuff finger-lickin' belly-bustin', lip-smackin' good
Can't seem to do without it
Some say, I like um lean and thin
Others like um short and fat
While still others savor um baking colored brown
Salted, smothered, and spiced
Still others say, just serve mine up unsalted, nice and plain
I even heard one say the other day
I likes mine big, fat, and greasy
And there are some few I've heard say
I'm taking mine home to mama
Or I'm full through and through and throwin' this bone away

Now, what does all that have to do with that good that happened
A long long time ago . . .

Well, Let me speak for a moment on this here . . .

The Word is . . . God created man
And from his rib fashioned woman
Breathed into them both the breath of life
Case y'all don't know or believe . . . that's in Genesis

And I'm here to tell y'all no matter how the woman
Is cut, cleaved, or covered
Shaped, sized, shaded, spiced, or smothered
Lean, thin and trim, short and drippin' with fat
Bubblin' brown, burnt black or baked barely brown
No matter . . . she's always . . . A-1 Prime Rib!
. . . And from the very beginning, I remind you,
God said . . . That's good!
Now mind y'all . . . you'd better treat her

Just like God said . . . Good!
And if'n you don't . . . those devil-fired ovens in hell
Are waiting just for you
And will pitch a fork and a fit.

Young Pretty Thang

Young pretty thang
Full of life, laughter and glee
Sporting not a care in this life
Spreading joy to any and all who
Will at her beck and call
Jump for her joy

One leap, full of fun
And condomedless liberty
A bridge to a shortened life
Extended by pain and shame
Steps away from a box
A hole, and a whole lotta loose grains
Of God's sparkling dust

Perhaps you shone and sparkled
For a little while on this side of the rainbow
But now you really have center stage
Within a cast of thousands of grains

If you can enjoy the brevity of this moment
And remember your opponent who is
Still free and at large
Full of life, laughter, liberty and glee
Spreading limited joy to another
Unsuspecting lover who will soon share
Your bed 'neath the sheet of earth's soil.

B's That-a-Way . . .

Why . . .
Black face
Broad nose
The look of royalty

Is everybody . . .
Big thick proud lips
Poetic utterings
Scholarly wisdom and wise
Nonsense and foolishness

Always . . .
Black wool-like hair
Styled down, fixed up
Real bad braids, afros
All kind-a curls swirls bangs and thangs

Looking at . . .
Big round shapely hips
On a fine, fine, fine frame

Staring at . . .
Bold beautiful big strong legs
Strutting, dancing, prancing
Running, jumping, winning gold medals

Why is everybody always looking
And staring at us

Honey . . .

Cause we're better looking than most
And you know what else . . . Honey . . .
It just B's that-a-way most of the time!

That's why everybody's always looking staring
And copying us!

Miss Jethued

Jethued is her name
Endowed she is with a fine fine ebony frame
She's big
She's pretty
But if you mess with her and ain't nice
She'll vex you, hex you, and
Might even put a spell on you
So watch out
Look out
No stuff she'll take
From you or anyone of a lesser hue
Oh yeah, less you forget
Call her Miss Jethued
And never ever by her first name or
Just plain Jethued!

I Love Me Some Shades of Beauty

I love me some Shades of Beauty
From the deepest and darkest ebony hue
High yellow, pale hues and every color twix and tween
Yes indeed, I loves looking at my Shades of Beauty
Dressed up, dressed down
Stockings grandmother style rolled down
Fixin up for a live Saturday night . . . hey baba re bop
Sunday morning *Amen!* pew
Lord have mercy, *Just a Closer Walk With Thee*
Amen and hallelujah too
Satin dresses house dresses high heeled pumps
Matching hats suede purses
Great big patent leather pocketbooks
Gloves and girdles, fur pieces, stoles, wraps,
Floor length coats, rabbit and mink
Girl . . . we can mix rabbit mink straw and silk
Purple and yellow, orange and red all at the same time
And come out, my sisters, togged down, dressed to kill
Smelling like integrated talcum opium and scented moth balls
My sisters, my sisters
Dior is the fool, don't all yall know
We can dress rings around Oleg Cassini,
Pucci Jeffrey Bean Calvin Klein and da de da de da
My sisters my sisters, yes, we have quite a flair
Style taste dash verve, trend and pace setters we are
We come in all sizes, shapes and forms
Big, little, tall, short, big buxom bootyful
Thin as a rail, plain Jane, sassy, foxy, sophisticated elegance
Black on black, single strand of milky white pearls
Bag ladies to bank ladies, shopping bags sewing kits
Attache cases, mops brooms lemon smelling dusting rags
Cleaning women church women
From hot knappy kitchens to salon treated,
Straightening combed permed hair
We can talk sensible play some dozens
Articulate with doctors and professors
Because we are doctors, lawyers, and all other kinds of professionals
We love the opera the symphony, plays musicals dirty home movies

From fun . . . . to fun loving . . . . to funerals
Lord have mercy, I do declare, Hallelujah too
False teeth, false hair, false nails, false lashes and false uh, uh, uh
False airs, we can take it off, put it on, leave it off, leave it on
Again, I do declare, give me some Shades of Beauty
Anytime, anyplace , anywhere
Dance hall, back seat, between the sheets
. . . *Baby Baby Baby, I got to have you for my own* . . .
Now, hey you all . . .
Don't make no mistake and tell us how to act
Cause we know, yes, we know, how to
Sho nuff, act up . . . sho nuff!
However, whenever, whatever
Shades of Beauty, we are some kind of good lookin
Good people, good women good sisters
No matter the religion, no matter the cost
No matter the tone, tint, hue,
No matter the size, big fat small skinny
The die is cast, we all in this together
So . . . baby, baby, baby,
We gotta stick together girl friend,
Cause we all fighting for the same peace!
In the same riot revolution life.

God's Natural Beauty Marks

Cows have big bulging eyes
Monkeys with their long slender tails are never a bore
Bees sting and make honey
Elephant's ears are huge and the nose a big long trunk
Rhinos with a sharp bone up front have the nerve to weigh several tons
Peacocks sport proud and colorful plumes
A giraffe's neck stretches almost to the moon
Ants are smaller than a minute
Zebras have stripes
Skunks stink and have stripes
Snakes have leathery skin and are proud of their tail's end
Leopard would never try to change their spots
Eels have electric shocks
Cats purr when they catch a long tailed mouse
Lions roar and donkeys bray
Each is proud and struts with pride
And enjoys their God-given beauty marks
My people . . . my people . . . my people
Why do we suffer our looks
Big lips, broad nose, hair that goes back
Frizzes, puffs up and some call bad luck
Skin - a color that is bold dark and black
That speaks to some in a foul language that says stay back
Broad but shapely butts that can capture anybody's look
And understand and shake to any tune
My people . . . my people . . . my people
Why do we suffer our looks
With tender thought and labors of love
God made me and you
Sized shaped and shaded us
Gave us the lips, the hair, the color and the butts
And then said . . . that's good
We can sing, we can dance, signify and play
Fly to the moon, write books
We can even change the way we look
So, why can't we be proud
Strut with our heads held high
Sporting splendor spirit and soul

And be happy with the way we look
Knowing that we too are
God's natural beauty marks.

That Woman

Petite pretty poised, so some say
While others say, vixen vain vile

And I say, how do they know?

The voices of several more, I've heard to say
Intelligent and witty
And what does she know
Sensitive sexy little witch
How does she rate

And I say, how - why do so many claim to know
Some say good . . . some say bad
Some utter words I dare not echo

And I say, Lordy, Lordy, Lordy
How do I maintain my sense of equilibrium
Or any kind of status quo

I remember and I quote, my dear old grandmother
You are blessed my dear little child just to be you

Be glad you are you, I do declare
'Cause the Good Lord created you
Knows every hair on your little head
And nobody, but nobody can
'Fess that 'tinction, not even you

But, I believe
You do know you
And nobody, but nobody
Can celebrate your fame
Nor even breathe what they think they
Might know 'bout you and your
Little old fine brown frame.

Willy-Nilly

I don't willy-nilly show what I got
No man needs to know what's neath my frocks
I can tell you tho'
It's a teasing and pleasing tan
Smooth, soothing, and soft as silk under glass
Sized, shaped, shaded and arranged just right
In all the best spots and places
Has the essence of come-on
But spells S-T-O-P in the name of LOVE
Cuz I'm a bonafide masterpiece of a woman
Delightfully designed and created by God
Whose attitude and fortitude
Says . . . Don't mess with my stuff!

The Versatility of Femininity is . . .

A fine brown frame illustrated with long black permanent press curls
Honoring such sweet sepia shades as
Caramel candy, butterscotch, chocolate chip and brownie mix browns
And the quiet brilliance of onyx and let's not forget
The mellowness of honey hush
Ruby red lips, long fire engine red finger tips, jeweled lobes
All of it, entertaining and exciting
The music and jive of Saturday night live
But on Sunday morning, it's all ala naturale
From head to toe, front and back
Big hat, patent leather pumps, bags to match
Singing praises and hallelujah amens from the front row pew

That, my friends, is the versatility of a sistah's femininity

Then comes Monday through Friday
It's a whole 'nother different look
Whatever her claim
Attache case, broom, stethoscope, etc., etc., etc.
A sistah's got what it takes to call the shots
Be the boss, fight for a cause
Whip sonny boy's butt
Comb and style braids in sistah child's hair
Study for the bar, shoot hoops
The lady is no tramp
You name it, she's got it
She can do it all in a heart beat
'Cause she's got that home-grown beauty
Created and fashioned by God from Adam's rib
Home-grown beauty from within.

All Those Various Shades

All those various shades of blacks and browns, like . . .
Coconut tan, black-eyes pea and peanut butter brown
Biscuit blushing teasing tan
Black pepper and the quiet brilliance of onyx
Inlaid ivory with tinted rose petal pink cheeks
The heart of darkness black, black, black
And every earth tone 'twixt and 'tween

The versatility of femininity
Is all God's various shades of black and brown
My sisahs, my sistahs,
Name your color
And wear it proud.

A Mess

She may not be the neatest; could possibly be the messiest
Her hair according to others never has a single strand
In its rightful place, and a woman was once heard to say
Oh, she has such beautiful hair if only she would comb and coif it
Her elbows sometimes smile a rusty shimmer and shine
And shyly blush with a tinge of radiant white chalky glow
The heels of her shoes are often worn, weary
Down and out, but comfort her soles
With the so-lace and contentment of inner peace
A peace that passes all understanding, and oh, my oh my
Her long sloppy baggy clothes, while claiming many spirited colors
Hide a multitude of greasy and candied sins
That coat and cover a little too fat, but fine bubbling brown frame
Everyday she carries at least three big, once beautiful bags
Each heavy laden and weighed down with everything
From a never-used comb, brand new rouge and makeup
To double AA batteries and even a few little lint balls
But, despite her unruly sight and even a desk at work
That seemingly bespeaks chaos and mess,
And some say needs to be dejunked . . .
Many people flock to her and walk and talk with her
People like sisters of the night, cellmates, shy little tots
And seniors whose faces are lined with wisdom and wit
They seem never to mind the litter, the clutter, and the
Persona of Pogo the packrat
'Cause they know that a long time ago
God breathed into her the breath of His life
Counted each hair and styled each strand in His place,
Blessed her ashy elbows, told her what to wear
And how not to worry about insignificant petty little things
And bade her to go out and mingle with the masses
Share her loaves and fishes and speak and act on His behalf
'Cause He knew exactly what was needed, where it was needed
And who He should call to be at His beck and command
And He never ever should be queried or questioned.

One-in-a-Million

There are more than a million good Black Men out there
Amen!
Uh . . . Amen! all by myself then
Do I hear the faint echo Amen of other sisters out there?
Come on sisters, stand up . . . speak out
I know yall know a whoooooooooole lotta good Black Men
Are they all low-down snakes, romping partying rascals
Good-looking devils, gay blades, preachers who love the three P's
Cellmates . . . crack cocaine cronies
Love-makin promising Romeos
Come on sisters . . . I know yall know several good Black Men
Naw, naw, naw, . . . not good-for-nothin . . .
But . . . good-for-somethin
Come on Black Pearls, no need to play and keep secrets
Games and hide-and-seek is for kids
I know yall know some good Black Males
Share the good news . . . right now
I'm sick and tired of singing and humming the blues
I know God didn't tend for me to world stage solo
I know yall know a few . . . a handful, two or three . . .
Just one extra one
I don't want yours, spill the beans sisters
Share the wealth; all I want is one!
Be a reference; tell him for me . . .
I will give him love joy happiness
All wrapped up in one little TNT package sealed with
A smile at sunrise, a hug at noon, a kiss at twilight
And in a crowded room, an extra special looooong wink
That silently speaks to him and says . . . here I am . . .
Take me, just little ole me . . . . . . all of me . . .
Sisters . . . Black Pearls
If this sounds like a plea
Uh . . . It just might be
I want a man! I want a Black Man!

Husbands

Husbands don't go to church
They don't make dolls
Nor do they cook, clean,
Wash, iron, mend,
Repair stuff or just talk

What then, do they do is the question I ask

They must be good for something
Let us stop in the name of love
Make a search and take a real good look

We know most of them love all the balls . . .
Football, basketball, baseball
And coupled with the couch and remote
They are as happy as if they had
Taken up permanent residence in paradise

Some say they are good for nothing
But I beg to differ with that
They are good for something
And if we keep on looking
Under the rug, under the welcome mat
Behind the sports and business pages
And not counting to ten
Perhaps trying some new places
Like the heart and soul
We just might find
Some good in them after all!

'Cause if they are with us
Day in and day out in comfort
. . . At the table
Sitting or snoozing on the couch
Detailing their car, or whatever
They must have already looked deep
Into our hearts and souls and theirs
Settled and made peace with that
'Cause after all we are the best!

Saturday Night Live

They make a beautiful couple on the dance floor
While her back end swings wide on turns
He kicks, but not too high
My, my, my
Big Mama and Big Poppa
Finger poppin'
At the Saturday night Live catfish fry
Whilst they swingin' and swayin'
To the rhythm and blues of the juke box
Everybody else is talking that jive and
Smacking on finger-lickin' bar-b-que.

Home Sweet Home

Home sweet home
A house full of waitin' and wantin' women and girls
Where have all the sons and men gone
A house full of women and girls
Little sis, big sis
Mama, granny, auntie, big mama and friendgirl
Living and working together
Sharing and caring, praying, churching
Struggling and raising little, innocent
Diapered babies and daddy-cravin' children
All under one roof
Life is for real, y'all
Where are all the black men
Remember . . . they used to be little overalled boys
Fightin' to lick mama's cake bowl
Playing games like marbles
Tryin' to be like cowboys, indians, and soldiers
Crouchin' behind the couch and on their bellies under the tables
Racing flappin' soled sneakers lickety split to home base
Pedalin' bicycles neck n' neck
Playin' cement ballgames, hide-n-go-seek between the
Door knob and the wall, and quickly jumpin' in and out of
Saturday night's hot sudsy bath
Then superfly and gangster rap,
Mimickin' video and cable sex
Life is for real, y'all
What happened to our little boys, bearing skinned-up knees
With the whistlin' wind tryin' to catch a runnin' nose
Beautiful brown faces and big inquisitive eyes, lookin' up
Dreaming to be big, havin' fun with a real ball
Then suddenly finding that life is not a game
But is for real, y'all
From skinned-up knees to sidewalk blood baths
Real hide-n-seek, a back billy-club seat covered
With real tears, planted dope and no hope
For real y'all, this is a life time deal
That can't be whipped or beat with black jack or twenty-one
Oh how I wish they were back

Living and dreaming life
Having fun in a home sweet home
Full of us women and girls
y'all!

Mirror, Mirror on the Wall

Mirror, mirror on the wall
Do I dare look into you at all
Fearing what I will really see
Rejected deep and depressed
Inside of me . . .

Is my life really a ball
Or am I due for a giant fall
If I should continue down this path
Entertained by pomp and circumstance
Instead of the Spirit's substance

Mirror, mirror on the wall
As I look and stare at my twin
I wonder who that image really is
Staring me up and down
Trying to tell me who I really am

Does my outside match my inner self
Or should I be turned inside out
Upside down and start all over again
Cuz' it seems I have nurtured
The outside to sprout and spread
Uncontrollably so . . .
Dispirited and disheartened
Into tall weeds and other dead stuff
While the undergrowth starves
For food and feed and a path to
Clear and clean air again

Mirror, mirror on the wall
As I experience the image of you,
My twin, can't you see I'm seeking
Help from the God within?

Thoughts to my Sister

Through the power of prayer
And everlasting faith
I endow you with my strengths
To use as you may
In your hours of need
As much as you may

And when you have used
As much as you need
Please return not to me
But pass on to a friend
Who may be in need

In this way
The cherished links
Of our true and unfettered
Sisterhood will never be broken

My Sister I love you!

HazelelizabethlillliecheeirmavelladolllizziecorineevanellLavernebettyjovoncillemah
jivancemakaylakendallshellyadairadajahchristiechriskhaliakanishatanishadarlaed
ythtashajessiesandralouisedeanaanayaminniemaelilllianartimeseloraellenrhodaka
therinemalissaconnieconstanceelieeleanorconstancevirginiabonnieannesuekaye
sthergloriamariechristineharrietlindaashantijacquelinejohnniemaeeversalindanicol
epathelenangelabeatricerebamarybrendavirginiacheecheerachaeltanyajoettalelali
sacarolejeannienatalielauriecandydoramaudiearmenterarlenalillietheomaelynnvic
toriaseawellowEdithgwendolynjeanjunerillastephaniediannmittiebeatricemarjoryir
enerebeccalouiseruthMildredythionediannannebeverlybarbararosemarylolamikkik
atiemariettadorthatheomaellenmarciajeanalleasjaninelisakarenmariedarenedarrita
marierolandasharonlynneleeannanadeansherylzeolareginaphylliskristajanievelma
floreenjessieIorettaleveniarenabernettaanitabrendaangelaantionettecamelladebra
cherimaryreneesusiejackiejudylelalilliemozellmelindamoszellleoliasheilarobinshir
leyminniejoannnancyfanniecarolynrosadebbierubyjewellesesnepatricepeggyemil
yclarahopehelencynthiagracelizziemaelouannienelliejunehazelmargaretemmabett
yjoycelougeniamarilynsammiegeraldinekathililliandeborahzeofiouscookieelouisei
damelanieverannanielisheydorothyleslietheImamarthacharleneodessamablepatri
ciashawnstaceyfrancestwiladoramalvinawilliepearlineleonavenusernestineanniec
hristinemelindatracypaulaaplislucillekarenidarebacecilianicolekatrinacharlottejud
ithbethjosephine̶n̶e̶i̶d̶a̶r̶a̶l̶a̶v̶e̶r̶n̶̶e̶k̶i̶m̶b̶e̶r̶l̶y̶m̶a̶x̶i̶n̶t̶a̶m̶a̶r̶a̶s̶h̶a̶r̶o̶nmahjililnarob
inpaulabonnies̶t̶e̶l̶l̶a̶r̶e̶g̶i̶n̶a̶s̶a̶v̶i̶o̶l̶a̶e̶l̶o̶i̶s̶e̶o̶l̶i̶v̶i̶a̶d̶e̶̶n̶i̶s̶e̶l̶e̶̶apanziegoldyne
stellareginalisaviolaeloiseoliviadeniseleolapanziesaranadagoldyneoleathatiffanya
gnessonyacalliecoralavernemahjijanicekathrynloisjohnnieflorenceangeleeberthac
armalethajrilorraineonedavirgielindanorawinonalenamalverbernicegloriaIululavivia
ndoriselaineveniceirmabessiedarleneprincesspaulinepennyveradorethabonniegra
cequeensusanjuanitamyrtlejosieritajanecheryloliveoliviarosettatreasureethellydial
oveymargueritedanamonamattiesuzettecarolroxannesandranolavoncillemakaylav
ernillaednamamiejuliecladairmakathleencelestinelillliealmaelmaelsiebillliecharlese
ttaelinoraloraellenrhodavaloniamargaretdeloresgladysjacquelineeleanorjettiearie
diannejozeldazellacamillealbertajevianpriscillaloistheolaelaineconsueloheatherja
ninemurielhenriettaasacarrieevelynkristineevaeveaccleconstancenormaandreatre
ssachelsealynetteserrenablanchedonnageorgiaanitaesthhersandyeddiemarianyol
andaclaudiachriswandadaisydoviephebealvasameliabonitacarmentanyadorafloss
ieriviannhattiesammielorettainasandragaylevaldagussieminniesabrinanellvickieeu
niceadrienneorebajeanetteaddiequanettabeckyaudreyelizabethsharonveronicavia
nnarlenaclaricelorileaheklaramichellejulieroselynmattiemariaaltaangelavaloriadar
lanaomiaugustajanicegertrudeceatriaelnorapamelavigeneolajeannieaprilloreneros
iedenisetsitsimonicaabigaildelphiamatrisnarvaleewandaviestaramonakristalonnie
pattykaysojournersadiephillisgwenmalverfreddierickoledawnvirginiaceceljessieh
arrietcolleenbeulahhannahkatricestarlacosundratrudygenevagenaysylviamartinan
elliegerthreenjuliadorcasdemetriadeborahfloradellaolivejoannamarjmalikaconniek
iangalauriesheliamagdalenemirianshebajemimahkaylacheyennephoebevashtiJoet
talelalisacarolejeannienatalielauriecandydoramaudiearmenterarlenalillietheomael
ynnvictoriaseawellowEdithgwendolynjeanjunerillastephaniediannmittiebeatricem
arjoryirenerebeccalouiseruthMildredythionediannannebeverlybarbararosemarylol

HE'S BACK

31

He's Black . . . .

He's black
Average size and frame
Short, cropped graying hair
Mid forties
Casual clean dress
Needs some dental work
Raised in a Christian home
Educated, talented

He's missing from family and home

This could be any mother's son
But he's mine
I love him and I miss him
As I'm sure any mother would

Please, let us pray for our sons
Let us pray that God will find them
Every single one
Inspire them to look up
Turn around
Come home
To family and friends

My heart is heavy
My home is lonely
But move on, I must
And pray that one day
Look up we will, and there
To our hearts' joy
Prodigal smile
Will be a mother's delight
Cause he's back!

Speak Up . . . .

I saw you a few minutes ago
Strollin' in the park
Dark shades on
Big brown bare legs

I just saw you a while ago
Now we meet again
This time in center court
Of the Grand Hotel

Togged down
High-heeled shoes
Long slinky black gown
Side sweep do
I know it's you

This time around
I'm gonna talk to you
Cause the last time
Couldn't think of a thing to
Say or do

Hello my Lady
The time is right now
Ain't shy no more

Hello, Miss Lady
This is no telephone line
I wanna see you and be with you
Let's sit right down
On this little settee

Our eyes meet
Smiles touch
Hearts unwind
Souls hum
Bodies be as one

We were meant to meet
Hearts to beat as one
Entwined in wine and roses
Live happily together
Forever chasin' rainbows on cloud nine

Juice

One
Two
Three
Here comes the tar

Four
Five
Six
Ready or not
Feathers flutter next

Seven
Eight
Nine
The rope is next

By the count of
Ten
Neck broke

The big hand has struck
The voice of death and doom
Rings loud and clear

Nigger! Nigger! Nigger!
Born a nigger
Die a nigger
Always a nigger!

Pretty Woman

pretty woman
contact blue eyes
spider webbed hair style

clad in a short tight dress
that's really a white sheet
in disguise

the kiss of death
is her smile

her arms
a hangman's noose
round your neck

her legs
long lean and lanky
are but stair steps
leading down to dust

brothers beware!

De Door

Every time de black man
walk out de door
maybe we see him agin
maybe we won't

Every time de black man
walk out de door
it used to be
noose and rope
now it's the man's dope

Every time de black man
walk out de door
and down the street
named wrong side
billy clubs and bullets
in de back and de head
they may be might meet

Every time my black man
walk out de door
say I love you papa
I love you sweet black honey
pray you gon
come back again
through dat door!

Mo Better Men

All you boys out there slouching on the corner
At the intersection of Short and Sweet, on
Dead End Street
All you boys who purport to be men
Boxing, sparring, dancing partners
With drinking, dope, doom and death
Skirting sin's edge
Claiming your masculinity through that
Which has captured and claimed your soul
Think it over, you boys who wanna be men
What . . . what are you commanding of yourself
And your sweet Ma'Dear
Ma'Dear who birthed, cradled, nursed you
With the bloody strength and depth of her livin'
Lovin' soul; think it over
You boys who purport to be men
You . . . you who tackled Ma'Dear
Tacitly snatching from her lode of love
Urgencies and luxuries for your very being
Borrow meant never paying back
Mother's Day was never even once a year
Your smile merely an illustrator's silent stroke
Your woman, your wh'women
Always held in higher and highest esteem
What this mounts to, sonny, in your vernacular,
Is pimping yo mama
Stealing deep from her pocketbook soul
Stressing straining sweet her last nerve
Little boys . . . counterfeit men . . .
Sons. . . in our love for you . . . we plead . . .
Heal us from this diseased cancerous sore
Named *boysnotmeninitis*
Grow up . . . little boys . . . be for real men
Breathing not on vain's festering ugly edge
Staying just one step ahead of
Sniffing barking bloodhounds
But etching deep yo life
Drawing on Ma'Dear's strong upbringing love

Carving a real blessing
Modeling for little craving hungry boys
Who declare themselves to be the
Epitomy of masculinity.

Through the Grapevine

I heard through the grapevine
That the quickest way to heaven
Is the next exit and the first right turn
And I said . . . My, oh my
I must detour and give that route a try
My friends, this is what I met
On my fast track to heaven

My new travel plan took me
Down through a rat-infested gutter
And an underground maze of chaos and clutter
I started my joyride
Dressed to kill and driving a long sleek hunk of steel
Joint in one hand, long stemmed crystal bubbly in the other
Nothing on sea, air, or land could stop me
I was luxury on a silver cloud, taking a shortcut to heaven
Going north, south, east and west
All at the same time
Flying high, looking low
Reno, Tahoe, Frisco, LA, DC, Atlanta, GA
Mapping my own geographical plan and plot

I laid a whole lotta fine brown frames
Smoked me some cocaine
Popped dope in my veins
Drank whiskey, gin, beer,
And ended with a big borrowed swig of wine
Slept my finery into sad rags on a cold pallet of cement
Played hide 'n seek with garbage cans,
Crushed cigarette butts, and stench
Need I say more . . . but let me finish with this
What I discovered on my rapid route
Was not a shortcut to heaven
But a nightmare in a quicksanded alley to
HELL!

So the next time you see a bypass sign
Or hear a grapevine tidbit

Be very cautious, canny, and careful
Check it out, my brothers and my sisters too
For you might find yourself in HELL, face-to-face
With sin, squalor, Satan
And me too.

Passage Rights

For too many
street-stretcher bodies
time and breath
oozing seeping
weeping out
bulging shocked eyes
split second seeing for the first
and last time
mother baby sister little brother
cornbread black-eyed peas
red beans and rice
tater salad bread puddin'
preacher church choir
black bow tie
where's my daddy
high school door books papers
drop out opportunity
repeating rifle
knock knock knock
blew it all slam open shut
dark side of night
street one block long
dim lights life blue notes
likker-drinking allies
crack cocaine cronies
street life greasy spoon
short sweet and sour
blood gushing spurting
spill and slop out and over
filtered blood stained tear drops
mustered up rainbow smile
one story another and another
rat race in the gutter
gone bye bye bye
green grass greener
man hole casket door sealed tight
six feet other under side
ta ta ta!

Fire Rages . . .

fire rages in a
black man's soul
burning and screaming
his heart raw
let me out
let me out

HazelelizabethlilliecheeirmavelladolllizziecorineevanellLavernebettyjovoncillemah
jivancemakaylakendallshellyadairadajahchristiechriskhaliakanishatanishadarlaed
ythtashajessiesandralouisedeanaanayaminniemaelillianartimeseloraellenrhodaka
therinemalissaconnieconstanceelieeleanorconstancevirginiabonnieannesuekaye
sthergloriamariechristineharrietlindaashantijacquelinejohnniemaeeversalindanicol
epathelenangelabeatricerebamarybrendavirginiacheecheerachaeltanyajoettalelali
sacarolejeannienatalielauriecandydoramaudiearmenterarlenalillietheomaelynnvic
toriaseawellowEdithgwendolynjeanjunerillastephaniediannmittiebeatricemarjoryir
enerebeccalouiseruthMildredythionediannanneberverlybarbararosemarylolamikkik
atiemariettadorthatheomaellenmarciajeanalleasjaninelisakarenmariedarenedarrita
marierolandasharonlynneleeannanadeansherylzeolareginaphylliskristajanievelma
floreenjessielorettaleveniarenabernettaanitabrendaangelaantionettecamelladebra
cherimaryreneesusiejackiejudylelalilliemozellmelindamoszellieoliasheilarobinshir
leyminniejoannnancyfanniecarolynrosadebbierubyjewellesesnepatricepeggyemil
yclarahopehelencynthiagracelizziemaelouannienelliejunehazelmargaretemmabett
yjoycelougeniamarilynsammiegeraldinekathilliliandeborahzeofiouscookieeelouisei
damelanieveranannielis**TICKLE**charleneodessamablepatri
ciashawnstaceyfrances**YOUR SOUL**leonavenusernestineanniec
hristinemelindatracypaulaaplisluciflekarenidarebacecilianicolekatrinacharlottejud
ithbethjoe...kimbermaxinemarsharanmahjililnarob
inpaulabon...tella...aloeloise...iader...anziegoldyne
stellareginalsaviolaeloiseviadeniseoleolapanziesaranadagoldyneolathatiffanya
gnessonyacalliecoralavernemahjijanicekathrynloisjohnnieflorenceangeleeberthac
armalethajrilorraineonedavirgielindanorawinonalenamalverberniceglorialulavivia
ndoriselainevenicereirmabessiedarleneprincesspaulinepennyveradorethabonniegra
cequeensusanjuanitamyrtlejosieritajanecherlyloliveoliviarosettatreasureethellydial
oveymarqueritedanamonamattiesuzettecarolroxannesandranolavoncillemakaylav
ernillaednamamiejuliecladairmakathleencelestinelillliealmaelmaelsiebilliecharlese
ttaelinoraloraellenrhodavaloniamargaretdeloresgladysjacquelineeleanorjettiearie
diannejozeldazellacamillealbertajevianpriscillaloistheolaelaineconsueloheatherja
ninemurielhenriettaasacarrieeevelynkristineevaeveaccleconstancenormaandreatre
ssachelsealynetteserrenablanchedonnageorgiaaanitaesthhersandyeddiemarianyol
andaclaudiachriswandadaisydoviephebealvasameliabonitacarmentanyadorafloss
ieirivianhattiesammielorettainasandragaylevaldagussieminniesabrinanellvickieeu
niceadrienneorebajeanetteaddiequanettabeckyaudreyelizabethsharonveronicavia
nnarlenaclaricelorileaheklaramichellejulieroselynmattiemariaaltaangelavaloriadar
lanaomiaugustajanicegertrudeceatriaelnorapamelavigeneolajeannieaprilloreneros
iedenisetsitsimonicaabigaildelphiamatrisnarvaleewandaviestaramonakristalonnie
pattykaysojournersadiephillisgwenmalverfreddierickoledawnvirginiacecceljessieh
arrietcolleenbeulahhannahkatricestarlacosundratrudygenevagenaysylviamartinan
elliegerthreenjuliadorcasdemetriadeborahfloradellaolivejoannamarjmalikaconniek
iangalauriesheliamagdalenemirianshebajemimahkaylacheyennephoebevashtiJoet
talelalisacarolejeannienatalielauriecandydoramaudiearmenterarlenalillietheomael
ynnvictoriaseawellowEdithgwendolynjeanjunerillastephaniediannmittiebeatricem
arjoryirenerebeccalouiseruthMildredythionediannanneberverlybarbararosemarylol

Her Poetry . . .

Her poetry
Will tickle your soul
And make love to
Your funny bone

My Pride and Joy

My pride and joy
Is peeking into the soul of the mirror
Past the permanent press curls
And the complexion's
Surface slick and smooth makeup
Straight into the heart of the matter
Beholding the true God
In me

Love is You

Even tho distance is our dance
And we cannot touch . . .

Our hearts
Are ever in faithful embrace
'Cause we are sisters
Who love each other
Very much.

One Way

Getting that kinda high
Is classified as
Living life too fast
In the one-way fast lane
Where speed races
Overtakes time
And assassinates
Punkish
Ignorance and innocence!

Chasin'

While we chase someone else's vision
In hot pursuit of that elusive pot-o-gold
Suddenly . . .

We are stopped
Dead in the midst of their
Superficial cosmetic
And sketchy realities
Bite the dust
Bid the day farewell
Kiss our future bon voyage
Come ashore
Full of ourselves
On the flip side
Of Mother Nature and
Her beautiful
Lilies in the field

The House is a Mess

The house is a mess
Kitchen sink piled high
Table full of papers and bills
No place for napkins and plates

My hair
Every single strand
Is in place, some place,
Out of place

My life it seems is all awry
Sons and daughters
In my pocket
As they get out of pocket

There is no husband
In house, in view,
Only way out of sight

What kinda picture is this?

Mixed . . .

You mixed alright . . .

With
tater salad
collard greens
fried catfish
hush puppies
red soda water
and tater pie
married
to your
big fat gut!

Innocence and Rage

Innocence and rage
Sometimes
Tar feather
And burn
Ropes trees
And crosses
Into the heart of
Mother Nature's soul

The Breath of Angels

The breath of angels
Play neath the future
Tickling and teasing
Hopes and aspirations
Sometimes prodding
Sometimes poking
But . . . ultimately
Inspiring
The sparkling dust of nature
Into star-dusted
Success

Human Waste Not . . .

Why waste time waiting
For a bouquet of roses
That may never come
For wonderful deeds
That you have done
When every thought you breathe
Is a seed ready to
Bud bloom and blossom
Into a glorious blessing.

The Morning's Sun

The morning's Sun
Colored Elusive
Peeks and pokes
Through
Graying white clouds
All the while
Winking and flirting
With me
And playing
Hide-and-seek
With Mother Nature Dear

Madam C. J.

The Madam would have a fuzzy fit
If she saw your hair
All fizzled unfried
Looking like
Wild black unsheared untamed wool

Never mind that your day
Is new wave now
Not the way of the hot iron comb
Sizzling the *do*
Smokin' and burnin' up
The kitchen too.

My Hair

My hair looks good
When it gets
Two weeks old
And thick!

Funny to the Bone

Your smile will laugh out loud
When the spirit tickles your soul
And your heart makes merry
With your funny bone

The Weeping Willow

The weeping willow sways
In the balmy evening breeze
And I say . . .

Pass my sweater please!

HazelelizabethlillliecheeirmavelladolllizziecorineevanellLavernebettyjovoncillemah
jivancemakaylakendallshellyadairadajahchristiechriskhaliakanishatanishadarlaed
ythtashajessiesandralouisedeanaanayaminniemaelillianartimeseloraellenrhodaka
therinemalissaconnieconstanceeelieeleanorconstancevirginiabonnieannesuekaye
sthergloriamariechristineharrietlindaashantijacquelinejohnniemaeversalindanicol
epathelenangelabeatricerebamarybrendavirginiacheecheerachaeltanyajoettalelali
sacarolejeannienatalielauriecandydoramaudiearmenterarlenalillietheomaelynnvic
toriaseawellowEdithgwendolynjeanjunerillastephaniediannmittiebeatricemarjoryir
enerebeccalouiseruthMildredythionediannannebeverlybarbararosemarylolamikkik
atiemariettadorthatheomaellenmarciajeanalleasjaninelisakarenmariedarenedarrita
marierolandasharonlynneleeannanadeansherylzeolareginaphylliskristajanievelma
floreenjessielorettaleveniarenabernettaanitabrendaangelaantionettecamelladebra
cherimaryreneesusiejackiejudylelalilliemozellmelindamoszellleoliasheilarobinshir
leyminniejoannnancyfanniecarolynrosadebbierubyjewellesesnepatricepeggyemil
yclarahopehelencynthiagracelizziemaelouannienelliejunehazelmargaretemmabett
yjoycelougeniamarilynsammiegeraldinekathililliandeborahzeofiouscookieelouisei
damelanieveranannielisheydorothyjalietbelma
ciashawnstaceyfrancestwilad

WHO
IS SHE...

gnessonyacalliecor... mahjij...
armalethajrilorraineonedavirgielindanorawinonalenamalverberniceglorialulavivia
ndoriselainevenniceirmabessiedarleneprincesspaulinepennyveradorethabonniegra
cequeensusanjuanitamyrtlejosieritajanecheryloliveoliviarosettatreasureethellydial
oveymarqueritedanamonamattiesuzettecarolroxannesandranolavoncillemakaylav
ernillaednamamiejuliecladairmakathleencelestinelilliealmaelmaelsiebilliecharlese
ttaelinoraloraellenrhodavaloniamargaretdeloresgladysjacquelineeleanorjettiearie
diannejozeldazellacamillealbertajevianpriscillaloistheolaelaineconsueloheatherja
ninemurielhenriettaasacarrieevelynkristineevaeveaccleconstancenormaandreatre
ssachelsealynetteserrenablanchedonnageorgiaanitaesthhersandyeddiemarianyol
andaclaudiachriswandadaisydoviephebealvasameliabonitacarmentanyadorafloss
ierivianhattiesammielorettainasandragaylevaldagussieminniesabrinanellvickieeu
niceadrienneorebajeanetteaddiequanettabeckyaudreyelizabethsharonveronicavia
nnarlenaclaricelorileaheklaramichellejulieroselynmattiemariaaltaangelavaloriadar
lanaomiaugustajanicegertrudeceatriaelnorapamelavigeneolajeannieaprilloreneros
iedenisetsitsimonicaabigaildelphiamatrisnarvaleewandaviestaramonakristalonnie
pattykaysojournersadiephillisgwenmalverfreddierickoledawnvirginiaceceljessieh
arrietcolleenbeulahhannahkatricestarlacosundratrudygenevagenaysylviamartinan
elliegerthreenjuliadorcasdemetriadeborahfloradellaolivejoannamarjmalikaconniek
iangalauriesheliamagdalenemirianshebajemimahkaylacheyennephoebevashtiJoet
talelalisacarolejeannienatalielauriecandydoramaudiearmenterarlenalillietheomael
ynnvictoriaseawellowEdithgwendolynjeanjunerillastephaniediannmittiebeatricem
arjoryirenerebeccalouiseruthMildredythionediannannebeverlybarbararosemarylol

Who Is She

Who is she
Source of life, holder of hope
Example for many
Honey . . . dripping sweet
She gives her very best
Expects your very best
Expects . . . much
At times too much
Who is she
Sincere simple wise
Helpful pushy at times
Elegant, simply elegant
Hours have no limits
Yours and hers
Everything has meaning
Everybody has purpose
She sees the smallest spot
Hears every little sound, a pin drop
Who is she
Woman wife
One and only
Ma'Dear to many
Auntie sister cousin
Granny big mama
Who is she
Look next to you
Look all around you
She is petite and pretty
Big buxom
Black and beautiful
Melted chocolate, Cococentric
She is being and breath
Standing on the edge of eternity
Clasping in her hands and heart
Seeds of life and creativity
Crying for you her children
All God's children to look listen learn
And leap into life with all faith

Into God's welcoming arms
Who is she
Look in the mirror
Believe . . . she is you.

Mama

In the beginning she carried me
When I was wee little and bitty
She carried nursed diapered bathed me
Washed and brushed my precious baby hair
She truly loved every little bitty ounce of me

As I grew older, she was always there
Talking with me, chiding me, talking bout boys n' girls
The things we should and shouldn't do
Definitely nothin' bout birds n' bees
But real life times and things

We talked bout school and books
Hairdos and curls and just plain girl talk
Church religion and God
Honey . . . we just talked bout
Everything everybody and all kinda things
She talked with me and at me
The smile in her heart was always there
Even when she fussed at me
I know she truly loved and cared for every bit of me

When I left the comfort of our home sweet home
Her door always waited open for me
The welcome mat even watched stretched and waited for
My children, their friends, and my friends too
Her table was always set with Sunday's linen and silvers best
The goodies she created and cooked made the whole house
Smell like kitchen heaven with aromas clinging to the walls
Floating out into all the other rooms and down the hall
If we didn't call or just drop in to visit and eat
Upset . . . she would really get upset

Now, this pretty little lady no longer dwells at our old house
Her door has been closed and locked for a while
But her heart is now at home in my heart
With her spirit abiding deep in my soul
Prompting my memory

Of a precious time 'tween me and she and all that we shared . . .
Kitchen table topics over iced kool-aid
The good times and the lean times

Now . . . believe you me
Today I model myself after this sweet gentle strong lady
Who birthed and taught me
Preached at me . . . healed . . . loved and cared for me
I'm really trying hard to be the same Mama to my children
Just like she was to me . . . and . . . just as hard to be the person
She tried so hard to teach me to be.

Mother's Day

Who is this lady . . . this woman
    we call mother

She is . . . miracle of generations
Breath of nations
Lady of the night
Goddess of dawn
Vein of life
    unworthy the pricking needles
    filled with man-made cancers
    eating away generations yet unborn

Today is Mother's Day
Who is this lady . . . this woman
    we call mother

She is God's smile
Answers to prayers
A haven in times of turmoil
Heart of gold
Arms that halo crisis before they unfold
A son's ace in the hole
A daughter's listening ear
Hubby's all around helpmate
Mother to her children's children
Teacher, preacher, doctor, lawyer, nurse
    disciplinarian . . . and the list goes on and on

Who is this lady . . . this woman

    Mother Grandmother Auntie
    Sistah Cousin Big Mama

She is love . . . our all in all

Today is her day . . .
Let us place
Upon her do, the Royal Crown of Everyday

Adorned with jewels of love, honor, admiration, respect
And dub her rich and rare
A beauty that was meant to be.

Metamorphosis

Love is . . . a day in spring
. . . . . Little girls
Bows and ribbons
Beaded braids and curls

Frilly fancy lacy white petticoats
'Neath ruffled dotted swiss
Layered checkered gingham
Shiny black patent leather shoes
With golden buckles

Little girls . . . are love
Sparkling twinkling eyes
Pretty puckered sugary lips
Lobes gifted with the brilliance of gold

Sweet little girls
Gold, silver, ruby, emerald delights
In God's crown

Little girls . . . flitter flutter fly
Curtsy to the dancing dawn
With a young lady's charm

Sweet sixteen
Flaming ruby red lips
Touched only by God's wand

Love is . . . . . a spring day
. . . . . Then . . . . as if by magic
Young women they become
Groomed in God's glittering
Gown of grace

Ah . . . . Spring is here
Mixing mingling mild fragrances
Whispering murmuring in the balmy breeze

Love is here to stay
forever and a day.

Tunnel of Time

In the ageless tunnel of Time
Bated and treasured breaths cloak and cling to
Minuscule molecules of the atmosphere
As they mix and mingle with the
Silver and gold threads of death
And the fragrance of wisdom and wise
Is floating around about waiting to be breathed
From heart to heart to heart
From soul To soul to soul

As we experience the ageless Tunnel of Time
We must live and breathe to our children
Our rites rituals traditions
Our culture and heritage
And the essence of all that is
Precious and dear to us

Yes, we must share these things with our children
Before the invisible glow and glare
Of the oncoming and precise mysterious light
At the Tunnel's end boldly focuses on us

And when that focus has captured
Claimed and wedded us as bride and groom to the
Fearless fate of that glaring mysterious light
The essence of all that we cherish and hold dear
For our children their children and generations yet unborn
Will still abide in the ageless Tunnel of Time
As minuscule motionless moments
Christened Rites Rituals Traditions
Culture and Heritage.

Touch

Today is a beautiful day
As I caress yesterday's memories
I relish the comfort of Mother's lap
The feel and forget-me-not
Fragrance of her bosom
Now wells up deep within my privacy
Her spirit kissing my tongue
Plants deep inside me
Tender irreplaceable thoughts
That silently and softly
Serenade and cradle my soul

The brilliance of
Mother's nature and essence
Brightens my heart
With a flaming torch
That flares, explodes and glows
Into my every breath . . .

Forget-me-not

In remembrance of me
This you do . . .

Touch your children
As I have touched you.

Big Mama

Big Mama
You've really made a difference
In the lives of so many
We pause here today
To pay tribute to you
Through sincere words from the heart
Smiles from the soul
Flowers from God's garden
We know from whence you came
And where you are now again
You have returned to the One
Who sent you to sit us
For this little while

Big Mama . . .
you made such a difference
In each of us . . .

And for this big difference
We thank our God
For sharing you with us.

Kismet

Cherry Blossoms in spring
Promising dimpled breasts
Blushing rosy round cheeks

Suns set
Flowers bloom
Dawns rise

A knight in shining armor
Stopped by one childlike morn
Kissed her kismet

She rose
Full bloom
Crimson glow

Graying lines
Wisdom and wise
Set and glow
Little girls no more

Change is Queen
Ruby red no more
But fertile still
Is soul and spirit
Born to flow and pass
From thence to eternity

HazelelizabethlilliecheeirmavelladolllizziecorineevanellLavernebettyjovoncillemah
jivancemakaylakendallshellyadairadajahchristiechriskhaliakanishatanishadarlaed
ythtashajessiesandralouisedeanaanayaminniemaelillianartimeseloraellenrhodaka
therinemalissaconnieconstanceeelieeleanorconstancevirginiabonnieannesuekaye
sthergloriamariechristineharrietlindaashantijacquellnejohnniemaeversalindanicol
epathelenangelabeatricerebamarybrendavirginiacheecheerachaeltanyajoettalelali
sacarolejeannienatalielauriecandydoramaudiearmenterarlenalillietheomaelynnvic
toriaseawellowEdithgwendolynjeanjunerillastephaniediannmittiebeatricemarjoryir
enerebeccalouiseruthMildredythionediannannebeverlybarbararosemarylolamikkik
atiemariettadorthatheomaellenmarciajeanalleasjaninelisakarenmariedarenedarrita
marierolandasharonlynneleeannanadeansherylzeolareginaphylliskristajanievelma
floreenjessielorettaleveniarenabernettaanitabrendaangelaantionettecamelladebra
cherimaryreneesusiejackiejudylelalilliemozellmelindamoszellleoliasheilarobinshir
leyminniejoannnancyfanniecarolynrosadebbierubyjewellesesnepatricepeggyemil
yclarahopehelencynthiagracelizziemaelouannienelliejunehazelmargaretemmabett
yjoycelougeniamarilynsammiegeraldinekathilillliandeborahzeofiouscookieeelouisei
damelanieveranannielisheydorothylesliethelmamarthacharleneodessamableapatri
ciashawnstaceyfrancestwiladoramalvinawilliepearlineleonavenusernestineanniec
hristinemelindatracypaaplifluckekaresidan bace nicolekatrinacharlottejud
ithbethjosephineoneidanarvalavernekimberlynmaxinetamarashannonmahjililnarob
inpaulabonniestellareginalisaviolaeloiseolviadeniseleolapanziegoldyne
stellareginalisaviolaeloiseoliviadeniseleolapanziesarahadagoldyneoleathatiffanya
gnessonyacallievo avieekayprincjohn lonceangeleeberthac
armalethajrilorraiveodeavirgedano vinoalenarariberniogglorialulavivia
ndoriselaineveniceirmabessiedarleneprincesspaulinepennyveradorethabonniegra
cequeensusanjuanitamyrtlejosieritajanecheryloliveoliviarosettatreasureethellydial
oveymarqueritedanamonamattiesuzettecarolroxannesandranolavoncillemakaylav
ernillaednamamiejuliecladairmakathleencelestinelillliealmaelsiebilliecharlese
ttaelinoraloraellenrhodavaloniamargaretdeloresgladysjacquelineeleanorjettiearie
diannejozeldazellacamillealbertajevianpriscillaloistheolaelaineconsueloheatherja
ninemurielhenriettaasacarrieevelynkristineevaeveaccleconstancenormaandreatre
ssachelsealynetteserrenablanchedonnageorgiaanitaesthhersandyeddiemarianyol
andaclaudiachriswandadaisydoviephebealvasameliabonitacarmentanyadorafloss
ieirivianhattiesammielorettainasandragaylevaldagussieminniesabrinanellvickieeu
niceadrienneorebajeanetteaddiequanettabeckyaudreyelizabethsharonveronicavia
nnarlenaclaricelorileaheklaramichellejulieroselynmattiemariaaltaangelavaloriadar
lanaomiaugustajanicegertrudeceatriaelnorapamelavigeneolajeanniaeprillloreneros
iedenisetsitsimonicaabigaildelphiamatrisnarvaleeewandaviestaramonakristalonnie
pattykaysojournersadiephillisgwenmalverfreddierickoledawnvirginiaceceljessieh
arrietcolleenbeulahhannahkatricestarlacosundratrudygenevagenaysylviamartinan
elliegerthreenjuliadorcasdemetriadeborahfloradellaolivejoannamarjmalikaconniek
iangalauriesheliamagdalenemirianshebajemimahkaylacheyennephoebevashtiJoet
talelalisacarolejeannienatalielauriecandydoramaudiearmenterarlenalillietheomael
ynnvictoriaseawellowEdithgwendolynjeanjunerillastephaniediannmittiebeatricem
arjoryirenerebeccalouiseruthMildredythionediannannebeverlybarbararosemarylol

73

Little Whispers

Little whispers
Are like the freshness of spring
Ushering in the
Cooling calm of a quiet summer breeze
After a light morning misting rain

Teeny tiny tots
Are like the
Dew resting on velvety petals
Whispering sweetness to each thorn
And loving the fragrance till dawn

Little tottling whispers
Are a mystery
That takes a lifetime to unfold

Little ones
Reaching out with whimpers and cries
Pleading tell-tell please
With their big inquisitive eyes
Lay that doping smoking pistol down
And let peace begin with
Me!

God Planted a Seed

God planted a seed a little while ago
It was watched and watered
By loving hearts and hands
The little seed grew and grew and grew
Into exquisite floral foliage
Its scent was spirit-filled
And an inner glow radiated outward
Touching many hearts and spreading much joy

Some cared and loved the little seed
Some played child-like games with the bud
Others enjoyed the blossoms
Still many many others
Were touched by its graceful and glorious bouquet

Then one day God said
Little seed, what a blossomed beauty you are
Your smile beams indelible blessings
On all you see and touch
Today the essence of your love
Has blushed day into twilight
Soothed your time into my heart of night
'Tis now your season to wither unto Me
And come home my little flower dear to Me

While weeping may endure for a night
The essence of the flower's aura
Will rise each misty morning blue
Basking in the Son's glow
Radiating in the ageless tunnel of time
With the lingering joy of an unforgettable fragrance
That we shall simply call
Precious Memories!

Before Our Very Eyes

Before our very eyes
The stage for a
Budding flower is set

The story unfolds
With the scene of frost on the pumpkins
And dew on the roses
And a lovely young lass
With feet poised to slide into
Slippers of delicate glass

The slippers can crack and break
The frost and dew evaporate
But if careful, the essence of both
Will blossom and glow
Day will fade into eventide
And midnight will not hide from thee
But will be the mystic hour of
Our young lass blossoming
Into a lovely single stem rose
With an attar that will last for an eternity.

Happy Birthday to our little girl
Who has grown
Into a lovely young lady.

Once Upon a Time

Once upon what seemed a long time ago
While dancing atop my daddy's toes
To the rhythm and melody
Flowing from his heart and soul
I dreamed success in all
That I would do
'Cuz he said I could be whatever my
Little heart desired
If I would in my childhood days
And in my youthful ways
Work and study before I played
And pray before I lay me down to sleep

That was when I was a wee little bitty girl
Dancing atop daddy's toes
Now I'm all grown up
Still work before I play
And now pray throughout the day

'Cuz of daddy's love and tender care
Not such a long time ago
I am an overnight sensation
Caressing daddy's teachings
Deep in my heart and soul
And still I dream and will do whatever
Lights up my heart
'Cuz God and daddy'
Loved me so very much
And danced with me
Quite some time ago

Baby Angels

God sends baby angels
Allows us to name, play with
And raise them
When they grow up
Some go their separate ways
Others do really wonderful and fantastic things
Some don't quite grow well at all down here
And return unto God to romp and play
With their little winged friends
Along the milky white way

But you my dear
Came from two of God's best
You're part of us
And we a part of you
We're all family
And that's no mistake

You are God's little miracle in motion
Our pretty little lady growing up
We're all here to help you do your very best
'Cause we all love and care for you a whole lot
And pray God's very best for you
As you dance the dance of angels
On this side of God's rainbow.

HazelelizabethlilliecheeirmavelladolllizziecorineevanellLavernebettyjovoncillemah
jivancemakaylakendallshellyadairadajahchristiechriskhaliakanishatanishadarlaed
ythtashajessiesandralouisedeanaanayaminniemaelillianartimeseloraellenrhodaka
therinemalissaconnieconstanceeelieeleanorconstancevirginiabonnieannesuekaye
sthergloriamariechristineharrietlindaashantijacquelinejohnniemaeversalindanicol
epathelenangelabeatricerebamarybrendavirginiacheecheerachaeltanyajoettalelali
sacarolejeannienatalielauriecandydoramaudiearmenterarlenalillietheomaelynnvic
toriaseawellowEdithgwendolynjeanjunerillastephaniediannmittiebeatricemarjoryir
enerebeccalouiseruthMildredythionediannanneberverlybarbararosemarylolamikkik
atiemariettadorthatheomaellenmarciajeanalleasjaninelisakarenmariedarenedarrita
marierolandasharonlynneleeannanadeansherylzeolareginaphylliskristajanievelma
floreenjessielorettaleveniarenabernettaanitabrendaangelaantionettecamelladebra
cherimaryreneesusiejackiejudylelalilliemozellmelindamoszellleoliasheilarobinshir
leyminniejoannnancyfanniecarolynrosadebbierubyjewellesesnepatricepeggyemil
yclarahopehelencynthiagracelizziemaelouannienelliejunehazelmargaretemmabett
yjoycelougerlamarileenmiegeraldinekathililliandebazeefiousookieelouisei
damelanieverasheydorohylesettaamarachaleodessamablepatri
ciashawnstacefrancesiadoraawillaarmilellsenanusenestineanniec
hristinemelindatracypaulaaplislucillekarenidarebacecilianicolekatrinacharlottejud
ithbethjosephineoneidaaneaveberlynaneshannonmahjililnarob
inpaulabonniestellazainaolaeoiseniseleolapanziegoldyne
stellareginalisaviolaeloiseelviadeiseleolapanzaesaragoldyneoleathatiffanya
gnessonyacalliecoralavernemahjijanicekathrynloisjohnnieflorenceangeleeberthac
armalethajrilorraineonedavirgieinanamalverberniceglorialulavivia
ndoriselaineveniceirmabessiearlenecessulinepennyveradorethabonniegra
cequeensusanjuanitamyrtlejosieaecoliveoliviarosettatreasureethellydial
oveymargueritedanamonamattiesuzettecarolroxannesandranolavoncillemakaylav
ernillaednamamiejuliecladairmakathleencelestinelilliealmaelmaelsiebilliecharlese
ttaelinoraloraellenrhodavaloniamargaretdeloresgladysjacquelineeleanorjettiearie
diannejozeldazellacamillealbertajevianpriscillaloistheolaelaineconsueloheatherja
ninemurielhenriettaasacarrieevelynkristineevaeveaccleconstancenormaandreatre
ssachelsealynetteserrenablanchedonnageorgiaanitaesthhersandyeddiemarianyol
andaclaudiachriswandadaisydoviephebealvasameliabonitacarmentanyadorafloss
ierivianhattiesammielorettainasandragaylevaldagussieminniesabrinanellvickieeu
niceadrienneorebajeanetteaddiequanettabeckyaudreyelizabethsharonveronicavia
nnarlenaclaricelorileaheklaramichellejulieroselynmattiemariaaltaangelavaloriadar
lanaomiaugustajanicegertrudeceatriaelnorapamelavigeneolajeannieaprilloreneros
iedenisetsitsimonicaabigaildelphiamatrisnarvaleewandaviestaramonakristalonnie
pattykaysojournersadiephillisgwenmalverfreddierickoledawnvirginiaceceljessieh
arrietcolleenbeulahhannahkatricestarlacosundratrudygenevagenaysylviamartinan
elliegerthreenjuliadorcasdemetriadeborahfloradellaolivejoannamarjmalikaconniek
iangalauriesheliamagdalenemirianshebajemimahkaylacheyennephoebevashtiJoet
talelalisacarolejeannienatalielauriecandydoramaudiearmenterarlenalillietheomael
ynnvictoriaseawellowEdithgwendolynjeanjunerillastephaniediannmittiebeatricem
arjoryirenerebeccalouiseruthMildredythionediannanneberverlybarbararosemarylol

WE LAUGH
AND WE
CRY

We Laugh and Cry

We weep
Experience pain, joy and grief

A tear
Captures claims
Imprisons so much

It lingers gently on the lid
Pooling thoughts
And then quietly spills over
Tumbles drops and falls

Escaping and splashing into a
Ranting raging torrential
Sobbing storm
A quiet calming ecstasy
Erupting with delight
Into a cascading waterfall
Washing down made up and false faces
Painting on cheeks the glistening gleaming glow
Of a blessed event
Smiling the mystique of moonlight and roses
Catching the carousel ring of a child's laughter
Coated with popcorn and cotton candy

A tear captures claims collects so much

A dream
Breath
Death

A tear can carry
Just so much!

Bussing

Kissing a diapered and dimpled baby
Is like touching quiet angel's breath
It has the hush hush of love and tenderness

Then there is the first love of sweet sixteen
Boy likes a girl, girl blushes boy
Their junior high kisses play merry-go-round
Ring around the roses, hide-and-go-seek
With bubble gum and red hots in the back seat
And turn to cotton candy as their freshman kisses
Seemingly have fun tickling tongues

Bride and groom bashfully whispering
To have and to hold, to love and cherish
And those famous last words
I do and then, till death do our lips part
Never once realizing . . .

The snare is being baited
For to catch and claim the
Endangered species
That's where the old marrieds
Just do it every now and again
When the moon is blue
Just to see if the touch's tingle and torch
Is still magic, tried and true.

Then there's Judas
Need I say more than it's just
Kiss, show, tell, and sell.

There do be other kinds of bussings
One stop . . . picking up more than two
Mixing and mingling spittle
Constantly crowding and jamming in more
As if there were no tomorrow

Where does your buss
Start and stop?

Roller Coaster

Life is a roller coaster and a merry-go-round
High up high and way down hades deep
Round and round and round
A drunken spree
It's so easy getting on
But getting off can be
As scary as a bug-a-boo
And coming down like
Landing in a bed of rocks
And steel-pointed nails

Life is a roller coaster and a merry-go-round
A candle burning at both ends
A long stemmed crystal goblet
Full of wine, women, and gaiety
Pop goes the cork, out flows the spill
Life on the rocks
A roll of the dice
The luck of the draw
What's in it for me
Monkey on my back
Somebody else's money on my crack
Day-old cigarette butts and ashes
Whiskey, beer, and wine flavored breath

How do I end this track
What price to pay
Bullet in the back
Knife in my gut
Heart of darkness
Compurgator with sin
Grave is my pallet

Whose name do I take as I try to end this mess

Lord, Lord, have mercy
On this my wounded and insulted life
Save me from myself, share with me the ring

Help me off the roller coaster
And the merry-go-round
That I started all by
My little self-centered self

Lord, I need your help!

Black

Anguish grief
Degradation deprivation discrimination
Trials tribulations
Heartache headache Weariness worriation woe

Bearing brown fatherless babies
Cellmates not helpmates
No hope . . . just dope

BLACK

Every Saturday night live
Kin against kin
Easter-filled pews
Lord have mercy

BLACK

You know and I know
BLACK ain't easy

BUT
If I had
A real nother chance
I know, I know, I know
I would be born again
Imaged and hued of earth
Just lak the Good Book say

Ebony-hued
Bold and beautiful
Strong as the butterfly
Companioned with doves

Free as the wind
Committed to the cause

BLACK, BLACK ain't easy

But it is . . . .
A RICH and RARE EXPERIENCE!

Guess what?

A child seemingly grown will trip, stumble, fall, and stray
And engage in the same sorts of games,
Things, and play they've seen
Screen-portrayed and otherwise dramatized
Failing to realize that these animated scenes will traumatize
And are nothing but betrayals, beckoning them
To do wrong, not as they ought and not as they were taught
And after action-packed series of don't do rights,
Some will come home before the dusk settles into dark
But some others will wait until right after dark
Still for some others, the darkest hour is just
Before the dawn
But the gloom has already bloomed
Into headaches and heartaches for
Way too many mamas and daddys

But, they are our children
The doors we must leave ajar
Some may try to sneak in and hide between
The door jamb and the wall
Others will be washed and flooded in by great big tear drops
And others will see the welcome mat and
Walk broadly grinning through the door big and tall
Extra baggage and babies
As if nothing had happened at all

Yes, they are our children
We taught them right from wrong
Trained them up Solomon said
And the apron strings we cut

My my my
looking back
did I too, do any of that
And as a parent
Did I willingly take them back
Or refuse to accept their call?

Saying What You Mean

Waltzing with words is something we all do
We may even mince a word or two
Misplacing a verb, dangling a participle
What's the difference between hello and howdy-do
Okey dokey and yes, I do
Playing games like hide and seek with this, that, these and them
Do we really say what we mean or what we think we mean
Is there one person lending an ear
Or more than two
Achild, an adult, or the little one inside of you
Do we really say what we mean
Or do we rarely say what we mean
Are we chatting, enjoying a gabfest, rap session, or
Merely shooting the breeze
Does yelling or screaming get in the way of
What we really think we mean
What about muttering, stuttering, stammering
Trite phrases - you know what I mean
You know, you know, you know, you know
Or just a look
And allowing the attitude to sing the tune
A nod, which way the head shakes, handshake
A gesture or just the whole body's moods and moves
There is so much mixed up in saying what we mean
Is there any wonder that the listener
Sometimes just looks wide-eyed, bobs the head up and down,
Moves on, drops your messages, doodles,
Perhaps naps, nods, snores and snoozes
Maybe even noshes and visits and disrupts neighbors
Hangs up, walks out, looks in amazement and moves on
To the next man, woman, child, group, or pet
To miscommunicate and even lead astray
Where do you see yourself in these few simple words
Singing and swaying with synonyms
Dancing, dodging, playing with puns
Pulling no punches
When you say what you say
Is it really what you mean to say

Or just what you think you might mean.
Or something that the casual eavesdropper
Can take delight and have pleasure in
Forget it and move on

Change Gon-a Come

Change is gon-a come
We all livin on the edge

Split second
Hair breath

Change is sho gon come

Why we so deathly
Opposed to thangs and change
Cause it sho gon-a come

One minute
Serenity and calm
The next . . .

Bombs burting in air

Change is gon-a come
We all livin on the edge

Sho nuff
Sho nuff!

Soap Opera

Life is like a soap opera
Changing yet still
It's time telecast in a smoky and smoggy test tube
Draped noosely in black and white hate crimes
And instead of curiosity knocking
My heart is peering and peeking in
Flashing before my very eyes, I see
People and places shifting
Changing sexes and traditional institutions
Children slaying children
Babies dying at the hands of babies
Too many bodies pillaged, liquored and all cracked up
There are unwanted and unwarranted fondlings taking place
From pulpit to pews to president
This is a celebrity-mad culture
Competing for a brief moment of fame and fortune at any cost
Many are running, seeking shelter from the winds and rains
That are woven into mighty patterns of devastation and destruction
Lord have mercy . . .
Even the weather is guilty of gusting and replacing pleasure with pain
Time is the only thing we can be sure of
There will be a tomorrow and there was a yesterday
And we even abuse that
Ladies and gentlemen, we are a time bomb
Set and ready to go off . . .
Lives and generations are at stake

People - mamas and daddies, children, people . . .
Stop in the name of love
Wake up . . . for the heart of the matter is this . . .

Let's capture this fogged up test tube
And cage it in its own time capsule
So that we can start dealing and pushing
The right stuff

Listen

Listen to our children, hear what they have to say
It wasn't too long ago that we were their age also
Sometimes it's tough for them
Oft times, it even very very rough
You must have some inkling of what it's like . . .
Let's look at what's mixing, mingling, and brewing in their pot
The pressures of dating and mating, and perhaps babies
Getting good grades, flunking, and incompletes
Maintaining a good attendance rating
Skipping, slipping, and just barley sliding by
Wanting to, but not knowing how to share
And ask questions of parents
Trying to understand the pain of
Mom and dad's divorce, sickness, and even death
Keeping up with the latest fads and fashions
Moods, money, movies, music, and
The mystic and magic of after midnight
Homework, housework and part time work
Academics and athletics
Clubs, committees, and commitments
Dances, drugs, dope, and cigarette smoke
Fights and feuds, gangs and guns
Sibling pressures and rivalries
No you can't . . . yes you can . . . maybe . . . I don't know
Perhaps a sulking silence as they come through the front door
and leave immediately by the back door
Come on parents, loosen up
Listen with your heart to what your children have to say
They are growing up, you know
They have beards and breasts; they aren't little anymore
With all this and more in their pots,
It's no wonder that sometimes they explode and blow up
It ain't all that bad, when you remember
What you did and what you had
It's not too much for you to respect their bodies,
Their language and their slang
It's just another passing stage, the play's the same
Only the name, the cast, and some of the circumstances have changed

And remember your famous last words . . .
If you don't, let me recall them for you . . .

When I have my children . . . this is what
I'm gon do . . . Do you remember the rest of that phrase . . .
I remember as thou it were yesterday . . .
All the pain, pressures, pleasures, and privileges
of being a teenager
Come on . . . Loosen up . . .
Give them a piece of your ear, a little of your shoulder
And some of your wisdom, wise, and wit
And listen too with love. . .
For they have lots to say

I Am My People

They will embarrass you, amuse and delight you
They will spark and ignite your imagination into words and deeds
Unimaginable

The colorful language and style of rapping and poetic talking
Will incite and influence your brain to come up with equal tales
Tete-a-tetes, and out-loud thinkings

Our colors dress up and put on new meanings
We constantly create our own style and vogue
Mixing and matching stripes, dots, plaids
Suspenders and sweaters, high platform heels and socks
Furs, hats, silks and cottons, caps and gowns . . . why . . .
The way we sport and romance our clothes, colors, and combinations
Brings all the sight seekers and copycats within
Walking distance of our communities, clubs, and churches

The hair thing . . Bo Derek got bold
With braids and beads and her people
Glowed with pride as they counted to ten
Grace Jones loooked good shaved bald and I even saw
One of them - uh ummmm, you guessed it - bald
Now don't that tell you something about who starts fads and things,
Who sets the pace and who bends the trends

The blues, jazz, skating and the jiving and the jamming
Proves we can be on the spot, think on our feet
And come out smelling like a flower garden
Full of roses in bloom

Our footwork coupled with the magical mystical movements
Between the shoulders and butts doing the slide, the glide,
The hully gully and the strut, demonstrates that we can work together
In synchronized perpetual motion
With any ballad, blues, be-bop, beeethoven or bach

All my people from the lightest and brightest to the darkest and blackest
The uncle toms, the thugs and the thinkers,
Color-coded passing misfits, sun-shaded red eyes
The bulging needle poking popping veined night owls and pimps

Ms. Society, the homeless, the helpless and
The short slit skirted ladies who day and night decorate and strut neon-lit streets
The least and the littlest, the tall dark handsome Romeos
Old cheating charley, my dear dad, the ma'dears, big mamas, aunties and sistahs,
These are all my people . . . and we are who we are

While our spirits lay claim to kingdoms in the sea
And castles in the sand, remember we survived Goree, the Middle Passage
And 400 years of slavery
We didn't get the 40 acres and the mule
But we built the towns and the cities
Developed original finger-lickin recipes
Nursed and raised our younguns and theirs
Manufactured their bedroom perfumes
And instilled delectable unforgettable aromas in their kitchens

We told them how to stop and go, how to sew and make shoes
We wrote the music and the songs, yes, even Dixie by Snowden
My people my people my people
Yeah, we got the rhythm, the moves and the blues
We were . . . . we are the movers and the shakers
The molders and the makers, blazing new trails
Underground and above ground
From the Arctic to the cow-poking, covered wagon trails of the west
Making a name for Lewis and Clark,
Laying groundwork and blazing paths for battles even now

My people my people my people . . . uh mmmmmmmmmmmmm
They will embarrass and amuse you, delight and enlighten you
They will even make you stand tall, smile and glow with pride and joy

Yes . . . my people, after all these years
I have finally come to realize that only my God knows why
From the first garden, including east of Eden
We have been maligned, murdered, manipulated
We stumble, struggle, spit, shoot, slander, slay each other
Smile and stab each other in the back, but still we survive

I am my people

Bridge

I sit
Pondering . . . wondering . . . speculating
I look to the east . . . to the west
To the north
And I still sit
Quiet
Considering . . . contemplating
Studying . . . surveying
Which way do I go
They stare cold and beady
Back at me
Ruthless
Cut throat
I dare you
But I not frightened
But bold and brave
With head held high
Look to the north
To friend not foe
And with arms outstretched
Take a calculated lead
The east . . . the west
And even the north
They have no other choice
But to follow my suit
And follow they do
Down that dead end and dreaded path
Right behind me
With my partner to the north in full pursuit
Ready to take over my charge
. . . . and lead the east and the west
Down that feared and frightful path
Where the door will slam
Shut! with a bang
And there really is no one to blame
Cause we have all the genius
Wisdom, wit, and brain!

Time

Time is still and silent
Speechless
Ceaseless, consistent, compelling
Given singly in equal precious portions to everyone
Taken for granted by many
It's as precious as 24 treasured jewels embedded
In bands of pure gold
It's a gleaming and a glowing with
The dust of nature's subtle power
It's pleasing and pressuring, passing
Time waits not for anyone
It's a tacit tick tock
Tick tock
Take it as it comes
One tick, one tock at a time
It's yours, granted by God from the beginning
With a choice for you . . .
To commit and become
Wedded to
Touched with aspiration
Or tipped with desperation
You may cooperate with it
Or try to control it
However . . . whatever ... whenever
The choice is yours
Use it as you wish
Remembering . . . it's silent
Ever moving
Each tick, each tock
Holding for us . . .
Dates with choices to make
Commitments to keep challenges to confront
Time is in your hands
Use it wisely
Or use it . . .
Up

We Wait

We wait all the time
For the right time
We say that night time is the right time
We promise that my time is your time
We declare that now is not the right time
We alibi and say I ran out of time

Now is never the right time
This is the last time
On this I will not waste my time
Of my life, I gave him the best time

Time is woven into every time
All we have is time
Unpromised time!

Focus

Today is that fork in the road
Where the dawn of decision looms . . .
Into a moment . . . an eternity

Whispering . . .
Touching trembling telling thoughts

Whispering. . .
Teasing taunting tempting thoughts

To the right
To the left
This way . . . that way . . . which way?

HARK!

Lean with your heart into the elusive wind
Focus on the spirit within
Stand on the precious promise

And . . . .

Today will your mansion be
The fork matters not
For the precious promise holds sway
When your path's focus
Is **God's Way**

Choices

Here . . . we stand on the threshold of life
Gateway of Choices

Through this portal all must enter

Up the stairs you can ascend
Or down the stairs
Stumble tumble descend

Either way the choice you must make
Invitations and temptations will abound

The challenge of that decisive moment
Can endure for an eternity!

You will need help in taking the right step
For many eclectic ones are around

The door is before you
Enter you must
Either way
Up or down . . .

The choice is yours to make!

One Night

One night as I was calmly catnapping
One eye half open, ears tuned to God
I thought I heard a little mouse
In my quiet and darkened house

As I continued to listen to God
I heard the little critter
Creeping and crawling
Around about and in my house
I know the wee critter is
Contemplating whether to have a festive celebration
With his chums when I'm out of my house

Hush! Hush! God was saying
Listen, the little brown mouse has a story
For your soul, let your heart take heed
Stop, listen, and look, take some action
Before mating season, and their time to breed

That little brown mouse, let's call him Henry
Comes out when it's dark and quiet
Checking and casing the joint
Taking curious cheer in all the
Cuisine, clutter, chaos, and confusion
That has captured your house
Listen to Henry
And My message will be crystal clear

Be still; be quiet;
Clean the cabinets, toss out the papers
Enliven your house with
The joy and excitement of creativity
Store your excesses in God's treasure chest
They'll not get lost, stolen, nor forgotten

Be still and be quiet
Listen and learn from Henry, the little brown mouse
Who has his sights set on claiming your house

Heed wee Henry's gnawed and silent message
Do what you gotta do and in just a little while
Henry will be out and about, and catered to by the
Cookies, crumbs, chaos, collections, and confusion
That are cluttering up your neighbor's house!

Lemonade Justice

In the heat of a mint julep night
As me and my sweet mama
Clad only in colored birthday suits
And enjoying the moon's delight
As it raided our sweltering romantic tete-a-tete
A loud bang, bang, bang
Interrupted the front door
And interfered with the back door
Without a word from me or she
The old blues rushed in
Grabbed and threw a choke hold on me
Knocked and spilled our long, tall drinks
And made them kiss the floor in front of us
The ice, lemons and sticky sugary water
Wet and wedded the floor
The old faded blues lost their cool
Excited a slip, slide, and glide and
Danced all around us . . .
To the beat of crash, bang,
Flying ice and broken glass
Me and my mama just laughed, jumped back
Watched flabby wildly flailing arms
Embrace our covered cement floor
And rednecks breaking down to the bone
As smilin' teeth flew high
Trying to find a home in the sky
Oh the old blues hully gullied, shook, rattled, and rolled
All over re-covering our floor
Oh sweet mama
While they wait for their ride in the pickup paddy wagon
Thanks for the iced lemonade you made for
Justus! to enjoy in the heat of the night
While loving the moon's delight

Too Many People

Too many people unlock their minds and
Use Satan's park and ride
They get aboard the redsuit's bus
Holding on for dear life and
Ride joy straight to hell's gate

The devil's pitchfork is the handrail
Slippery and greasy, it will always
Cause them to fail

Now we are told the devil has a tail
Long and deadly, it will stretch you to
Lie, cheat and steal
Then cut off your air
Keep you in a strangle hold
All the way to hell
Once you get their
Uuummmm.................... baby
There is no turning 'round!

So if you don't like
Fire, brimstone, and sweltering
All-the-time heat
Don't allow that devil
To incarcerate your soul
Keep yourself free
Don't unlock and leave your mind
In Satan's park and ride
'Cuz once he has your mind
The next thing he'll steal
Is your soul . . . the devil is a
First-class, natural rascal and rogue

The Medium Is The Message

Uh oh, there rings the telephone
But never you mind, the recorder is on
For you see, nothing interferes with
The matching and mating of my morning newspaper
With my coffee and cream

Uh oh, there goes the telephone
But never mind, the recorder is still on

And I need to take these few moments to
See and hear what's staring and stalking me from
Tthat television screen

Uh oh, there goes that telephone again
But that's okay, the recorder is still on

And nothing but nothing interferes when
I'm resting on my throne

Uh oh, there it goes again, and thank goodness
The recorder is still on

The radio is on, playing some real cool morning jazz
And I just gotta stay in this little room til Miles
Is finished and gone and besides that
My behind is still conferencing with the throne

Uh oh, there goes the telephone, yes, the
Recorder is still on, but let me run and try to catch this call

Hello . . . didn't quite make it, they gone
There it goes again . . . Hello
Who . . . No, wrong number!

Wow, there it rings again . . . Hello . . .

No, heavy breathing does not reside in my home. Oh shucks,
The caller ID simply says anonymous.

Well, that's enough of that . . . I really don't have time
To sit here and go through all of this . . .
Recorder, have fun, you get to take all the rest!

My Black History

This is Black History Month
An observance founded in 1926 by Dr. Carter G. Woodson

I ask the question . . .
Is there really a need to celebrate
Black History . . . and for an entire month

Why do I . . . Celebrate and observe Black History

I celebrate today because
I'm colored ebony and I'm extraordinary
I celebrate today 'cuz my heart
Is connected to the roots of Africa's Baobob Tree
Those roots represents my culture
Stretch, spread, and sprawl all the way
To the Tree of knowledge
And the Tree of Life in the Garden of Eden
My spirit's culture spreads up through its strong
Truck becoming one with the rich, lush, green foliage which
Gets its life and breath from the heavens
It is there that I stretch my hands to Almighty God
Say thank you, thank you for birthing me

I celebrate today for all my ancestors whose
Spirits are yet living in castles in the sand 'neath
The Baobob tree and kingdoms in the depths of
The ocean deep, in musty cellars, in bushes and undergrowth
Along invisible tracks of the underground railroad

I celebrate yesterday . . . I celebrate today . . . I celebrate tomorrow
My Black History is an extension of me
And everything I do bespeaks the love of my people
The honoring of my past and respect for our future

This is why I sing my life
It is a melody, a song unheralded
Each note is true, not blue
But black and beautiful
Sing your song; celebrate your life
Honor Ourstory

HazelelizabethlillliecheeirmavelladolllizziecorineevanellLavernebettyjovoncillemah
jivancemakaylakendallshellyadairadajahchristiechriskhaliakanishatanishadarlaed
ythtashajessiesandralouisedeanaanayaminniemaelilllianartimeseloraellenrhodaka
therinemalissaconnieconstanceeelieeleanorconstancevirginiabonnieannesuekaye
sthergloriamariechristineharrietlindaashantijacquelinejohnniemaeversalindanicol
epathelenangelabeatricerebamarybrendavirginiacheecheerachaeltanyajoettalelali
sacarolejeannienatalielauriecandydoramaudiearmenterarlenalillietheomaelynnvic
toriaseawellowEdithgwendolynjeanjunerillastephaniediannmittiebeatricemarjoryir
enerebeccalouiseruthMildredythionediannannebeverlybarbararosemarylolamikkik
atiemariettadorthatheomaellenmarciajeanalleasjaninelisakarenmariedarenedarrita
marierolandasharonlynneleeannanadeansherylzeolareginaphylliskristajanievelma
floreenjessielorettaleveniarenabernettaanitabrendaangelaantionettecamelladebra
cherimaryreneesusiejackiejudylelalilliemozellmelindamoszellleoliasheilarobinshir
leyminniejoannnancyfanniecarolynrosadebbierubyjewellesesnepatricepeggyemil
yclarahopehelencynthiagracelizziemaelouannienelliejunehazelmargaretemmabett
yjoycelougeniamarilysam...dina...illiand...ozeofiouscookieelouisei
damelanieveranannielishdoroth...elmamar...ac...neodessamablepatri
ciashawnstaceyfrance...loramalvina...ill...arle...avenusernestineanniec
hristinemelindatracypaulaaplislucillekarenidarebacecilianicolekatrinacharlottejud
ithbethjosephineoneidamarvalaverne...imb...rlyn...axinetamarashannonmahjililnarob
inpaulabonniestellareginalisav...el...oliviadeniseleolapanziegoldyne
stellareginalisaviolaeloiseoliviadenisel...apanziesarahadagoldyneoleathatiffanya
gnessonyacalliecoralavernemahjijanicekathrynloisjohnnieflorenceangeleeberthac
armalethaj...ora...eedav...l...hor...a...alverberni...orialulavivia
ndoriselai...l...mabes...are neprincess...lie...veraorethabonniegra
cequeensusanjuanitamyrdeposior...ajanecheryloli...oli...arose...a...eethellydial
oveymarqueritedanamonamattiesuzettecarolroxannesandranolavoncillemakaylav
ernilladednamamiejulieclíz...athi...o...estnelliealmaelsiebilliecharlese
ttaelinoraloraellenrhodaval...nia...argar...dio...ady...jacquelineeleanorjettiearie
diannejozeldazellacamillea...berta...evian...priscilla...st...laelaineconsueloheatherja
ninemurielhenriettaasacarrieevelynkristineevaeveaccleconstancenormaandreatre
ssachelsealynetteserrenablanchedonnageorgiaanitaesthhersandyeddiemarianyol
andaclaudiachriswandadaisydoviephebealvasameliabonitacarmentanyadorafloss
ieriviahattiesammielorettainasandragaylevaldagussieminniesabrinanellvickieeu
niceadrienneorebajeanetteaddiequanettabeckyaudreyelizabethsharonveronicavia
nnarlenaclaricelorileaheklaramichellejulieroselynmattiemariaaltaangelavaloriadar
lanaomiaugustajanicegertrudeceatriaelnorapamelavigeneolajeannieaprilloreneros
iedenisetsitsimonicaabigaildelphiamatrisnarvaleewandaviestaramonakristalonnie
pattykaysojournersadiephillisgwenmalverfreddierickoledawnvirginiaceceljessieh
arrietcolleenbeulahhannahkatricestarlacosundratrudygenevagenaysylviamartinan
elliegerthreenjuliadorcasdemetriadeborahfloradellaolivejoannamarjmalikaconniek
iangalauriesheliamagdalenemirianshebajemimahkaylacheyennephoebevashtiJoet
talelalisacarolejeannienatalielauriecandydoramaudiearmenterarlenalillietheomael
ynnvictoriaseawellowEdithgwendolynjeanjunerillastephaniediannmittiebeatricem
arjoryirenerebeccalouiseruthMildredythionediannannebeverlybarbararosemarylol

LOVE IS AN INCREDIBLE THING

Love is an Incredible Thing . . . .

You breathe it in the spring
When robins and blue birds cheer up
You sing it, you hum it, you look it
You like it, you love it
You sense it when the
Rains plip plop from a rainbow's blush
You smell it after a fresh summer bath and breeze

Love is a strange but wonderful thing

It's cutting the birth cord
A child coming home from school
A child going away to school
It's seeing and loving a child's big brown
Inquisitive eyes looking up at you
It's a little child's tears, hurts and skinned up knees
Being rocked to comfort on daddy's knee
It's knowing the dimples and feeling the acned pimples
And going through the teens age
Cutting the birth cord
Snipping the apron strings
A big person's blues

Love is strange and sometimes hurting and painful scene

It's the taste of birthday cake and ice cream
Candy kisses
Holding hands
Dancing in the moonlight
Wine and roses at twilight

It's in your heart, way down deep in your soul

It puts sparkle in your smile
Honor in your hug
Empathy in your embrace

It's a shoulder to lean and cry on

Praying for someone's mournful plea
Understanding a why, why, why
A questioning look, a silent appeal

Love is all these things and much much more
Love is a strange but miraculous thing!

Unspoken

From opposite corners of a crowded and gay soiree
Flirtatious searching eyes meet . . . shyly linger
Casting a mystic spell over tender thoughts . . .
Telling thoughts
Thoughts that softly touch
Quietly exploding into a spontaneous oneness

Two smiles meet and silently reveal and embrace
A million unspoken words . . .

      a fairy tale
      a fantasy
      a wish come true
      a love story
      secrets to be . . .

From opposite corners of a crowded and gay soiree
Eyes met and lingered
Thoughts and smiles
Captured and claimed it all

Two hearts . . . two souls
In one split second
Playfully and boldly orbit the moon
Nestling on Cloud Nine . . . a real natural high

The soiree has ended . . . but for two . . .

      . . . A New Beginning . . .

You

You were my knight in shinning armor

My prince charming too

How easy it was to say . . .

Yes, yes, yes,
I do, I do, I do
To you

For you were
My Dream come true

Balloons

Oh my dear heart
You are my life . . . you are my love

You mean so very much to me

You are like stars waltzing on moonbeams
You are the land of Make Believe
Where all my wishes
Dreams and fantasies
Come true

You are balloons
Red. . . yellow . . . green
Orange . . . blue

If I should pop them one by one
Each one would explode
With wine, roses, candlelight
And the very, very essence
Of You!

First

The essence
Of our first moment together
Is now a living memory
Etched in eternity

Ducky!

How do I love him, let me recount my ways
From the top of his little head
Down to the bottoms of his feet
And all that is twixt and 'tween
Allow me to declare what I like about my man

Every single strand of hair
'Round his ears and part way up his head
Even though knotted and kinked
Is good enough for me
His big brown eyes sparkle
His nose broad and brown
Sits perched atop big luscious, appetizing inviting lips
Even his jeweled ears are fit to be kissed

His chest is big enough to comfort
And frame little old me in peace and serenity
There's plenty good room for his
Chesty hairs to romp and play and dance
On my chinny chin chin
His muscular arms hold and embrace my whole self
Beneath our covers throughout the night
His little and big toes and my two big toes
Tickle, tease, chase, and play
Hide-n-go-seek, little Red Riding Hood,
And this little piggy
While my little toes silently and playfully
Scream, don't eat me! And let's get on with this undertaking
Between the sheets and the pillows 'cause this affair ain't no sham

His heart is big
His soul an unplumbed well of velvety rose petals
All of him is wrapped in deep brown tasty chocolate
Coated with sugar, spice, and everything that's nice
And it's all mine, ladies,
Waiting and wanting to melt and drip all over me

How do I love him, let me recount my ways

From the top of his clean shaven (bald) head
Down to his toes, jam, and soles
Including his heart and soul
I'm here to tell everybody
There is no mystery, intrigue, no secrets here
He's just ducky, and I'm just plain old lucky

Missed You Today

Today my thoughts were of you
I thought of your smile
And that little twinkle in your eyes

I thought about your body
Next to mine
A loving touch
So gentle and smooth
Just like aged wine

My thoughts were of you today
And all the little things
You do and say

Need I say . . .
Oh, How I missed you today

Corner in my Mind

There is a corner in my mind
Reserved for a very special person
It's cloaked and draped in secrecy
All lit up with lots of adoration
Its aura is effervescent and bubbly with
Excitement and glee

If its walls were to speak
The essence of my thoughts
Would shout out for all to hear

Oh my darling dear
My love for you
Is as deep and wide as all the rivers
Hot as the noonday sun
Twinkling and sparkling like stars above
Ready and waiting to walk on cloud nine

Oh my darling dear
If only I could live these dreams true
My days and nights
Minutes and hours
Would come alive
With every bit of you

Floating Fragrances

Floating fragrances of spring
Promenade prance and parade
In the crispy dewy morning air
Lingering long and lingering late
'Til long after the day has faded and settled
Into a quiet and peaceful solitude
Spirits and sprites gently
Caress our hearts with love and laughter
Our souls soar over the rainbow among the clouds
On a magic carpet of attar from a thousand rose petals
And each new day
Our love is a crisscrossed trellis
Intimately vined with
Sensuousness, happiness, ecstasy and joy
We listen with our hearts to the
Cherubic coos of two tiny love birds
Cradled in a soft slight spring breeze seemingly
Whispering . . . .
I love you, I love you, I love you

Ah spring . . .
A dream come true
A love story
A fairy tale

. . . . . Once upon a time
A kiss, I do, I do love you

And our love
Endured for a million spring times

This Precious Moment

This precious moment my thoughts border on you
My self strives to limit and fence you out
But memories and thoughts keep slipping through
What do I do
I ask me
I ask you
You have and hold the answer
Tacit though it may be
Your absence and silence
Ring loud and clear
You no longer hold any part of me
Heal and hope me now, I must
And get on with my keeping on
What is to be will be
And that does not embrace together
You and me
Rather - your one self as usual
Me - seeking that which will
Eventually come to be
One other to love
Have and hold
And be one with me

Abra Ca Dabra Presto

Raindrops prance and parade
Snowflakes flitter hither and yon
Flirting with the naked boughs of winter
Whilst beds and bulbs lie in comfort
Under the waiting rites of spring fragrances

And almost as quick as the blink of an eye
And the sound of the Magician's
Abra ca dabra presto
The harbinger chirps
The bees and butterflies
Waltz in the balmy breeze
To the tune of James Brown's
Please Please Please
The stars twinkle and
Play hide-and-seek with the
Clouds by day and
The man in the moon at evening tide
And come the dawn, the morning's breath
Serenades the dew on the velvet colored roses

My lover hands me a hankie
'Cause the pollen pops the question
And I, of course, just have to respond and react
With teary puffy eyes
Running nose red
And a spraying and a splattering of
Moisture from my lips that he calls
Teeny tiny little sparkling spit balls

Achoooooooooooooooooooo!

All Stood Up

When we couldn't stargaze in the park
You promised dinner for two
Anywhere I wanted to
Guess what . . . You stood me up
For that too . . .
You didn't show
Nor did you call
Now after several days hearing no word
I'm wondering if you'll ever show or call at all
Perhaps you will in a day or two
Or a few . . . years that is
Call with apathetic apologies
Frizzled flowers and maybe a trite little poem
But, Mr. So-and-So
Before you pick up your phone and call
I'm calling to tell you a thing or two
Listen . . .
What's a standup and a snub between friends
That can't be made up with . . .
Sparkling champagne and Mr. See's
Every week, a dozen American Beauties
Dinner and dessert at the Needle
A card and a promise started with Pretty Please
I'll never stand you up or snub you
In this life again!

You and Me

After a long and tiring day at the office
Home we come to our domain, through the front door
Attache cases in hand, headed for our thrones
You in the love seat and me
In the big soft leather reclining easy chair
We are ready, you and me, to bask in the
Quiet and solace of our togetherness

Especially me, your hubby dear, I'm ready
For the quiet touch of our lips touching cheek to cheek
Kissing away the memory of Old Hard Lips
Spewing spit balls as a blessing out he gives me

Yes, me too, Precious Dear,
I'm good and ready for your loving arms
To encircle and hug me, smothering out the memory
Of my counterparts and competitors sabotaging
And attempting to outsmart me

Yes, Indeed, we are both primed and ready for
A few kind words to drown out all the
Hassling, haggling and office politics
I'm glad you're home dear
Slip into your negligee and slippers
Sink into your special love seat
Sip this little glass of cool juice
That I've poured just for you
Read the paper, rest and relax
Watch a little TV or listen to some kool jazz
I'll have your candlelight dinner ready
In just a shake and it won't be shake-and-bake
Rather it'll be your favorite petite filet mignon steak

After dinner, leave everything to me
I'll clean our plates, wash the dishes,
Straighten things up, so that you can get ready and not be late
You know we have a standing midnight date

Just me and you every single night
And after we turn out the light
Do our thing and say goodnight
Just remember, tomorrow night is your turn
To bring my paper, my slippers and robe,
Pour me a cool jug of juice
Broil my favorite T-bone steak,
Clean and straighten up everything and turn out the lights

After all, we are a team Working together and aiming to please
Me and you Baby, Just me and you . . .
All the way Everyday in every way!

HazelelizabethlilliecheeirmavelladolllizziecorineevanellLavernebettyjovoncillemah
jivancemakaylakendallshellyadairadajahchristiechriskhaliakanishatanishadarlaed
ythtashajessiesandralouisedeanaanayaminniemaelillianartimeseloraellenrhodaka
therinemalissaconnieconstanceeelieeleanorconstancevirginiabonnieannesuekaye
sthergloriamariechristineharrietlindaashantijacquelinejohnniemaeversalindanicol
epathelenangelabeatricerebamarybrendavirginiacheecheerachaeltanyajoettalelali
sacarolejeannienatalielauriecandydoramaudiearmenterarlenalillietheomaelynnvic
toriaseawellowEdithgwendolynjeanjunerillastephaniediannmittiebeatricemarjoryir
enerebeccalouiseruthMildredythionediannannebeverlybarbararosemarylolamikkik
atiemariettadorthatheomaellenmarciajeanalleasjaninelisakarenmariedarenedarrita
marierolandasharonlynneleeannanadeansherylzeolareginaphylliskristajanievelma
floreenjessielorettaleveniarenabernettaanitabrendaangelaantionettecamelladebra
cherimaryreneesusiejackiejudylelalilliemozellmelindamoszellleoliasheilarobinshir
leyminniejoannnancyfanniecarolynrosadebbierubyjewellesesnepatricepeggyemil
yclarahopehelencynthiagracelizziemaelouannienelliejunehazelmargaretemmabett

GUEST POETS

Bernard Harris, Jr.

Harold Murphy

hristinemelindatracypaulaaplislucillekarenidarebaceceilianicolekatrinacharlottejud
ithbethjosephineoneidamarvalavernekimberlymaxinetamarashannonmahjililnarob
inpaulabonni
stellareginalisa
gnessonyacalliecoralavernemahjijanicekathrynloisjohnnieflorenceangeleeberthac
armalethajrilorraine
ndoriselaineveni
cequeensusanjuanitamyrtlejosieritajanecheryloliveoliviarosettatreasureethellydial
oveymarqueritedanamonamattiesuzettecarolroxannesandranolavoncillemakaylav
ernillaednamamiejuliecladairmakathleencelestinelilliealmaelmaelsiebilliecharlese
ttaelinoraloraellenrhodavaloniamargaretdeloresgladysjacquelineeleanorjettiearie
diannejozeldazellacamillealbertajevianpriscillaloistheolaelaineconsueloheatherja
ninemurielhenriettaasacarrieevelynkristineevaeveaccleconstancenormaandreatre
ssachelsealynetteserrenablanchedonnageorgiaanitaesthhersandyeddiemarianyol
andaclaudiachriswandadaisydoviephebealvasameliabonitacarmentanyadorafloss
ieirivianhattiesammielorettainasandragaylevaldagussieminniesabrinanellvickieeu
niceadrienneorebajeanetteaddiequanettabeckyaudreyelizabethsharonveronicavia
nnarlenaclaricelorileaheklaramichellejulieroselynmattiemariaaltaangelavaloriadar
lanaomiaugustajanicegertrudeceatriaelnorapamelavigeneolajeannieaprilloreneros
iedenisetsitsimonicaabigaildelphiamatrisnarvaleewandaviestaramonakristalonnie
pattykaysojournersadiephillisgwenmalverfreddierickoledawnvirginiaceceljessieh
arrietcolleenbeulahhannahkatricestarlacosundratrudygenevagenaysylviamartinan
elliegerthreenjuliadorcasdemetriadeborahfloradellaolivejoannamarjmalikaconniek
iangalauriesheliamagdalenemirianshebajemimahkaylacheyennephoebevashtiJoet
talelalisacarolejeannienatalielauriecandydoramaudiearmenterarlenalillietheomael
ynnvictoriaseawellowEdithgwendolynjeanjunerillastephaniediannmittiebeatricem
arjoryirenerebeccalouiseruthMildredythionediannannebeverlybarbararosemarylol

Bernard Harris, Jr.

Described once as "bold and brilliant," Bernard has been writing poetry for over 20 years. Born and raised in Philadelphia, Pennsylvania, anger was initially what motivated Mr. Harris to write. He now believes poetry may have saved his life, as he used it as "therapy," especially during his years in the military. Today his writing is inspired primarily by a desire to provoke thought and to promote unity in the community. A full time writer/poet, Bernard resides in Seattle, Washington.

Last Nite

Inspired by Morresia Johnson

When emotion overwhelms reason, it denies the words
To explain. Again confusion causes a quiet storm and
I am lost by your side.

Nothing could be said to ease my rage, so what could
Be done? Sometimes I scare myself and I have to step
Out to call time-out to realize where I am.

Crossroads cause conflict from every corner. My
Decision to continue is not an easy one - but one based
On survival, and happiness, and you.

None of which do I find in my brief screech of solitude,
In the midnite offshore breeze,
In my anger and indecision.

Solemn in my return and warmly welcomed by your embrace,
A silent confirmation, at last by your side.
Forever, where I belong.

My Lady's Birthday

Today is my lady's birthday
And I'm too far out at sea.

Seems my whole life's been underway
Could never stay where I wanted to be.

Today is my lady's birthday
I miss her in my arms.

Still I feel her when I'm away
I'm wrapped up in her charms.

Today is my lady's birthday
Physically. We're not together.

It's a spiritual love I would say
I know things are getting better.

Today's my lady's birthday
Reminding me of fine wine.

If I had words then I would say
She's tasting sweeter all the time.

Today's my lady's birthday
And soon . . . we will be as one.

It's not too much of a price to pay
Because our love is second to none!

Peaceful Evening

Last night the phone rang…. I think.
  Someone knocked
on my door two
  or three times.

Outside I heard a friendly blow
  right beneath
my bedroom window,
  just after the screaming sirens
had just died off into the distance.

I believe I heard about some bad news
…….in and between some
meaningless commercials
and the illest be-bop-hip-hop-non-stop
rap record around…. on the radio.

Fortunately,
  the only one I let in
was you!

When Jamilah Smiles

For my daughter Marita Jamilah

As we try to keep things in their proper order,
we just told a bedtime rhyme to our new baby daughter,
and to see her peacefully sleeping, well there is nothing
greater. So leave your message now, and we'll talk to you
later.

An answering machine message, perhaps a little misleading
because we could be in the middle of a late-night feeding.
and realizing our new lifestyle comes completely into focus
when we see our Jamilah smile.

Inheriting the wisdom of Walker, the beauty and brains of
Bethune and the strength of Tubman, leading the righteous.
My Marita Jamilah, mother of man, born with royalty just
like Isis.

Some say it's bound to happen, you will definitely be a
daddy's girl. That may be true because my pledge to you is
all the love in the entire world.

Who would have thought, after ten years together, our lives
would be blessed to get so much better. A whole new world is
certainly undersaid, because I cannot remember the last full
night's sleep in my bed!

Still I am thankful for a dream come true, born to us a little
princess, bringing joy like no other. The very essence of
innocence, looking just like her mother. Smooth cocoa skin
and superior style, it all comes together when we are graced
with Jamilah's smile.

It's hard to believe, my sweet little brown bundle of sunshine
turning upside down this life of mine. Without a doubt the
best thing to happen in a long, long while. . . .
and I thank God for my Jamilah's smile.

Harold Murphy

Harold H. Murphy is a native of New Orleans, Louisiana. He has self-published three poetry books. In his third book, *Grasses of the Sunshine*, Murphy introduced a triad verse style that he has given the name "Murphisms."

Murphy has resided in the Seattle, Washington area for more than twenty years during which time he has served as the Poet Laureate of the Black Community Festival of Seattle, was a columnist for the oldest African-American newspaper in the State of Washington and was an active member of the Afrikan-American Writers Alliance of Seattle. His two other poetry publications are *Murphy Moments and Sparrow in the Wind*.

For Her To See

by Harold Murphy

> As I look into
> my little girl's eyes . . .
> I wonder if . . . I pray that . . .
> she sees . . . in my eyes . . . what I see . . .

Coretta King . . . a rock strength carrying unbearable sorrow and pain
Tina Turner . . . a whirlwind song of unbridled freedom
Rosa parks . . . a quiet undeniable power

> Images in my eyes . . . as I look into
> my little girl's eyes . . . and . . . I wonder if . . .
> I pray that . . . she sees . . . what I saw . . . in my eyes

Shirley Chisolm . . . cutting the uncut edge
Moms Mabley . . . shedding all claims to shame
Wilma Rudolph . . . looking never back

Images of my past . . . that spoke for me . . . that now speak for her . . .
and . . .
I wonder if . . . and . . . I pray that . . .
she sees . . . what I saw . . . with my eyes

My #1 Soul Sister Momma of unbelievable unbreakable faith
Her #1 Soul Sister Granny of unconquerable universal love

I WIDEN MY EYES TO REVEAL ALL FOR HER TO SEE . . . AND . . .

I look with wonderment . . . into . . .
My little girl's eyes . . .

I see My future . . . in her eyes
I see Your future . . . in her name . . .

I wonder if . . .
I pray that . . . she sees . . . what . . .
she was named . . . to be! . . . . . . You see

My little girl's name is . . . **DESTINY!**

Always There

I Remember . . . Her
Always Beside me
Never Behind . . . Sometimes
ahead . . .

Slave ships
Cotton fields
Underground railroad

I Remember . . . Her
Always Beside me
Never Behind . . . Sometimes
Ahead . . .

Protests
Riots Jail

I Remember . . . Her
Always Beside me
Never Behind . . . Sometimes
Ahead . . .

Emancipation
Liberation . . .

Always Beside ME
Never Behind . . . Sometimes
Ahead . . .

I REMEMBER HER . . . **BLACK WOMAN ALWAYS . . . THERE!** . . .

Uncut Jewel

Sapphire Sister
Wears her pants
like a mister

Sapphire Sister
spits a burning acid
spins like a twister

Sapphire Sister
boldly stands alone
no one to kiss her

Sapphire Sister
loves with no give
her love a killer

Sapphire Sister
truly love yourself
your drama just a thriller

Sapphire Sister
let your God give you peace
let your pain finally cease

Go away . . . Go pray . . . Don't delay!
And then . . . . . . when you return . . . . .
Soul-full Sister   . . Please stay!

Be a heaven lit gem . . . shine our Way!

The Original

Black Woman of the Original Seed . . .
  A Divine Mission . . . God
  Has given Her . . . to show without a doubt . . .
  Divine unwavering Wisdom
  Divine undeniable Power
  Divine uncompromising Passion . . . to show without a doubt . . .
  Supreme Divine Love

Black Woman of the Original Seed . . .
  You have born . . .
  The first beginning of humanity
  You have born . . .
  the middle-passage of inhumanity
  You will birth . . .
  The last breath into heavenly glory

Black Woman of the Original Seed . . .
  A Divine Mission . . . She
  Must keep
  all faiths . . . She
  Must overcome
  all hurdles . . . She
  Must resist
  all temptations . . .

Black Woman of the Original Seed . . .
  A Divine Mission . . . Her
  Heart is to keep
  the beat . . . Her
  Soul is to lift
  the spirit . . . Her
  touch is to ease
  the pain . . .

Black Woman of the Original Seed . . .
  You are why . . . All Women must bleed . . .
  You are why . . . All Humanity will succeed . . .
  You are Mission Divine!

THE MOTHER of THE ORIGINAL SEED

About The Author

LaVerne C. Williams Hall
Mother, Grandmother,
Great Grandmother
Doll Artist
Poet, Artist, Preacher
Teacher

A native of Austin, Texas, she grew up and was educated in Portland, Oregon. The Seattle, Washington area has been her home now for more than forty years.

Hall is an ordained Baptist preacher and serves as the Assistant Pastor at a local Baptist Church in Seattle, where she is in the primary stages of developing a Christian Women's Institute. Her collection of original poetry, stories, and sermons are based on real life experiences. An original line of greeting cards she developed over the years are sent primarily to family and friends.

Other books include, *The Quiet Brilliance of Onyx*, *Hair's What it's All About, My Little Mahji Paper Doll Series*.

Hall has five adult children, seven grandchildren, and two great grandchildren. A world traveler, her most enjoyable trips have been to South Africa.

www.ingramcontent.com/pod-product-compliance
Lightning Source LLC
Chambersburg PA
CBHW020442290526
45785CB00002B/969